I0002280

Smart Cities and AI

How Artificial Intelligence is
Transforming Urban Living A Look at
IoT, Data Analytics, and AI in City
Infrastructure

Greyson Chesterfield

COPYRIGHT

DISCLAIMER

The information provided in this book is for general informational purposes only. All content in this book reflects the author's views and is based on their research, knowledge, and experiences. The author and publisher make no representations or warranties of any kind concerning the completeness, accuracy, reliability, suitability, or availability of the information contained herein.

This book is not intended to be a substitute for professional advice, diagnosis, or treatment. Readers should seek professional advice for any specific concerns or conditions. The author and publisher disclaim any liability or responsibility for any direct, indirect, incidental, or consequential loss or damage arising from the use of the information contained in this book.

Chapter 1: Introduction to Smart Cities and AI

Overview of Smart Cities and How AI Fits In

In today's fast-paced, rapidly growing world, cities are grappling with the challenges of urbanization, resource management, and sustainability. The global urban population is projected to reach 68% by 2050, according to the United Nations. With this surge, cities are increasingly adopting technology to improve the quality of life for their inhabitants. Smart cities, powered by cutting-edge technologies like Artificial Intelligence (AI), the Internet of Things (IoT), and data analytics, are transforming the urban landscape to better manage resources, optimize infrastructure, and create more livable environments.

A smart city is not just a buzzword; it is a fully integrated, interconnected urban system that leverages advanced technologies to solve complex problems and improve the efficiency of various city functions. Smart cities utilize AI to make sense of massive amounts of data collected from sensors, devices, and citizens. By using this data effectively, cities can optimize services, enhance public safety, and promote sustainability. AI is the driving force behind this transformation, enabling cities to learn from past events, make decisions in real time, and predict future trends.

In this chapter, we will explore the key technologies that make smart cities a reality, the role of AI in this transformation, and how AI can be used to address the challenges cities face today. We will also discuss real-world examples that show how AI is already being implemented in smart cities and the potential for even greater advancements in the future.

Key Concepts: AI, IoT, Data Analytics, and Automation

To fully appreciate how AI is shaping smart cities, we need to understand the fundamental technologies that support them. These include AI, IoT, data analytics, and automation. Let's break these concepts down.

Artificial Intelligence (AI)

AI is a branch of computer science that focuses on creating machines capable of performing tasks that would typically require human intelligence. These tasks include decision-making, problem-solving, pattern recognition, and learning from experience. In the context of smart cities, AI is used to process and analyze large volumes of data to make intelligent decisions. Whether it's predicting traffic congestion, detecting patterns in energy consumption, or optimizing waste management systems, AI provides the computational power needed to handle complex urban systems.

AI algorithms can be divided into two categories: **narrow AI** and **general AI**. Narrow AI, the most common form today, is designed to perform specific tasks, such as analyzing traffic patterns or detecting security threats. General AI, on the other hand, is a theoretical concept where machines have the cognitive abilities to perform any intellectual task that a human can. While we are still far from achieving general AI, narrow AI is already making a significant impact on urban management.

Internet of Things (IoT)

The IoT refers to the network of physical devices, vehicles, sensors, and other objects that are embedded with software and sensors to collect and exchange data over the internet. In a smart city, IoT devices are spread across the urban environment, constantly generating data. This data could be from traffic sensors, smart meters, air quality monitors, and even citizens themselves through their smartphones.

IoT is essential for creating smart cities because it enables real-time data collection and communication. For example, traffic lights equipped with IoT sensors can detect the number of cars at an intersection and adjust the traffic flow accordingly. Similarly, smart buildings can use IoT devices to monitor energy consumption and adjust heating, ventilation, and air conditioning (HVAC) systems for optimal efficiency. Without IoT, the vast amounts of data needed to make a smart city work would be impossible to gather and process.

Data Analytics

Data analytics is the process of inspecting, cleaning, transforming, and modeling data with the goal of discovering useful information, drawing conclusions, and supporting decision-making. In the context of smart cities, data analytics plays a crucial role in transforming raw data into actionable insights. The data collected by IoT devices, sensors, and other sources must be analyzed to extract patterns and trends that can be used to improve urban services.

For example, data analytics can be used to track traffic flow and identify congestion hotspots. By analyzing historical data and real-time traffic information, city planners can make informed decisions about where to build new infrastructure, how to manage traffic, or even when to schedule road maintenance. Data analytics can also be used in healthcare, public safety, and environmental monitoring, among other areas, to improve the overall quality of life in a smart city.

Automation

Automation refers to the use of technology to perform tasks without human intervention. In smart cities, automation is used to streamline processes and improve efficiency. AI and automation go hand in hand: AI algorithms analyze data, while automation tools act on that data to perform tasks. Automation can be seen in traffic management systems, energy grid management, waste collection, and even in managing city services like water and sanitation.

For example, smart traffic systems can automatically adjust the timing of traffic lights based on real-time data about traffic volume, reducing congestion and improving traffic flow. Similarly, waste management systems can automatically schedule trash collection based on data from IoT sensors in trash bins, ensuring that garbage is picked up efficiently without the need for manual intervention.

Benefits of AI in Urban Living: Improving Efficiency, Sustainability, and Quality of Life

The adoption of AI in smart cities brings numerous benefits that improve the efficiency of city operations, promote sustainability, and enhance the quality of life for citizens. Let's explore these benefits in detail.

1. Improving Efficiency

AI can make city operations more efficient by automating repetitive tasks, optimizing resource use, and providing real-time data for decision-making. For example, AI-powered traffic management systems can optimize traffic flow, reduce congestion, and minimize fuel consumption. In cities with dense traffic, this can lead to significant improvements in travel time, air quality, and energy consumption.

AI can also be used in energy management. Smart grids powered by AI can predict energy demand, adjust supply accordingly, and reduce waste. This means that cities can ensure a more reliable energy supply while lowering costs and reducing their carbon footprint.

2. Promoting Sustainability

Sustainability is a key goal of any smart city, and AI plays a pivotal role in achieving this. With AI, cities can better manage resources such as water, energy, and waste, making them more sustainable in the long run.

AI algorithms can optimize water usage by detecting leaks and predicting future water demand based on weather forecasts, consumption patterns, and other factors. In terms of waste management, AI-powered systems can sort recyclable materials more efficiently, ensuring that waste is diverted from landfills and recycled properly.

AI can also be used to monitor air quality and reduce pollution. For instance, AI algorithms can analyze data from air quality sensors to identify pollution hotspots and suggest actions such as adjusting traffic patterns or regulating industrial emissions.

3. Enhancing Quality of Life

AI can greatly improve the quality of life for city dwellers by providing more responsive, efficient, and personalized services. AI-powered systems can improve healthcare services by predicting disease outbreaks, analyzing medical data, and offering telemedicine solutions to remote areas.

Additionally, smart cities use AI to enhance public safety. AI can be used to predict crime patterns, analyze surveillance footage, and provide law enforcement agencies with insights to prevent crimes before they occur. AI-powered emergency response systems can also help reduce response times and provide first responders with critical information in real time.

Real-World Example: AI in Smart Traffic Management Systems

One of the most impactful applications of AI in smart cities is in the field of transportation. Traffic management is a complex task, especially in large cities where congestion and inefficiency are common problems. AI is playing a crucial role in transforming traditional traffic management systems into smart, adaptive systems that can respond in real time to changing conditions.

A real-world example of AI in smart traffic management is the use of AI-powered traffic lights in cities like Los Angeles, San Francisco, and Singapore. These cities have implemented systems that use AI to control the timing of traffic lights based on real-time traffic data, collected from cameras, sensors, and GPS systems. The AI algorithms analyze traffic flow patterns, congestion levels, and the number of vehicles at each intersection, adjusting the traffic light cycles accordingly to optimize traffic movement.

For instance, in Singapore, the Land Transport Authority has deployed an AI-based system that adjusts traffic signal timings dynamically to improve traffic flow. The system is connected to thousands of sensors across the city that collect data about vehicle speeds, traffic volumes, and other conditions. By processing this data in real time, the system can adjust signal timings to reduce congestion and improve traffic efficiency.

In addition to improving traffic flow, AI-powered traffic systems can also reduce emissions and fuel consumption. By optimizing traffic light timing and reducing idling time, these systems can help reduce greenhouse gas emissions and improve air quality.

Another example is the use of AI in autonomous vehicles, which are becoming a critical part of smart cities. AI-powered self-driving cars can communicate with traffic lights and other vehicles in real time, allowing them to navigate more efficiently and reduce traffic congestion. In the future, autonomous vehicles could be integrated into the broader smart city ecosystem, working alongside other AI-powered systems to create a seamless, efficient, and sustainable transportation network.

Chapter 2: The Building Blocks of Smart Cities

Components of Smart Cities: Infrastructure, Governance, and Technology

A smart city isn't a single monolithic system; rather, it is a sophisticated, multi-layered ecosystem built upon three core components: infrastructure, governance, and technology. Each plays a critical role in enabling a city to operate efficiently, sustainably, and in harmony with its citizens. Understanding the integration of these components is essential to unlocking the full potential of a smart city.

1. Infrastructure

At the heart of any smart city lies its infrastructure— the physical and organizational structures necessary for the operation of urban life. This includes roads, bridges, public transport systems, water supply, sewage, and energy networks, to name just a few. But in the context of a smart city, infrastructure extends far beyond the traditional realm, integrating technology to create adaptive, responsive, and self-optimizing systems.

Smart Infrastructure

Smart infrastructure involves integrating sensors, data analytics, and automation into the built environment. For example, sensors embedded within roadways, bridges, and buildings can continuously monitor the health of the infrastructure, detecting signs of wear, corrosion, or structural shifts before they become critical problems. In cities like Amsterdam, smart streetlights not only provide illumination but also gather data on air quality, temperature, and motion, feeding that data into centralized management systems.

Furthermore, smart grids are transforming the way electricity is distributed and consumed. Traditional power grids, which distribute electricity from a central point, are being replaced with smart grids that allow for bidirectional communication between utilities and consumers. These grids can dynamically adjust supply based on real-time demand, reducing energy waste, improving efficiency, and even supporting renewable energy sources.

Building Sustainable Infrastructure

Sustainability is a key objective in modern urban planning. The integration of renewable energy sources, such as solar panels, wind turbines, and hydropower, into a city's infrastructure helps reduce its environmental footprint. Smart cities employ technology to manage and monitor the energy grid, ensuring that resources are used efficiently. This includes real-time monitoring of energy consumption, predictive maintenance, and automated adjustments based on weather patterns or shifts in demand.

A perfect example is the city of Masdar in the United Arab Emirates, where the infrastructure is designed to minimize energy usage and maximize sustainability. The city's architecture uses natural cooling techniques, such as wind towers and reflective surfaces, while renewable energy is harnessed from solar and wind sources. The integration of IoT-enabled sensors and AI systems allows the city to continuously optimize energy efficiency.

2. Governance

While infrastructure provides the backbone of a smart city, governance ensures that the city's resources and systems are managed effectively and ethically. Governance involves the policies, regulations, and practices that guide decision-making and the administration of the city's services. In a smart city, governance is directly connected to data-driven insights, which help local governments make informed decisions and improve public services.

Data-Driven Governance

The advent of AI and data analytics has transformed governance from reactive to proactive. Local governments are no longer waiting for problems to arise; instead, they are using predictive models to forecast issues and implement preventive measures. AI systems can predict traffic congestion, analyze environmental data to mitigate pollution, and even assess public health risks by monitoring social media posts, news articles, and public health records.

For example, in Barcelona, AI-driven systems are used to monitor traffic patterns, manage waste disposal, and track energy usage. The city collects data from thousands of sensors scattered throughout the urban environment, then applies machine learning algorithms to make decisions in real-time. For instance, if an area shows signs of increased pollution, the city can adjust traffic flows or enact air quality improvement measures on the fly.

Citizen Engagement

Governance in a smart city is also deeply connected to citizen engagement. Smart cities leverage technology to foster a deeper connection between the local government and its citizens. Mobile apps, online platforms, and social media provide residents with the ability to give feedback, report issues, and participate in decision-making. In the city of Helsinki, Finland, citizens can access a mobile app that allows them to submit real-time data on city infrastructure or environmental quality, which is then used to inform local policies.

Moreover, participatory governance can be enhanced through blockchain technology, which ensures transparency in the decision-making process. Blockchain can be used to track the usage of public funds, record transactions, and manage contracts, fostering trust and accountability.

3. Technology

Technology is the driving force behind the smart city movement, enabling innovation, connectivity, and efficiency. The integration of advanced technologies into the fabric of urban environments is what truly distinguishes a smart city from a traditional one.

The Role of IoT and Sensors

At the foundation of smart city technology lies the Internet of Things (IoT). IoT refers to the network of physical devices embedded with sensors, software, and other technologies that allow them to connect to the internet and exchange data. These devices range from smart streetlights to air quality sensors, from traffic cameras to water meters.

Sensors embedded in various parts of the city enable real-time data collection, making it possible to monitor everything from traffic flow to waste management and energy consumption. These data streams are invaluable for city planners and government officials, providing them with the insights they need to optimize city services and resources. In Singapore, for example, the government has integrated over 1,000 IoT sensors across the city to monitor air quality, traffic patterns, and waste levels, which helps in real-time decision-making.

The Role of AI in Smart Cities

Artificial intelligence takes the data collected from IoT devices and transforms it into actionable insights. Through machine learning algorithms, AI can identify patterns, make predictions, and automate processes that previously required human intervention.

AI can be used in a variety of smart city applications. For instance, in traffic management, AI-powered systems can process real-time data from traffic cameras, sensors, and GPS devices to predict traffic congestion and adjust traffic light timings accordingly. In energy management, AI systems can analyze usage patterns and dynamically adjust energy distribution to optimize consumption and reduce waste.

AI-powered systems can also be used for predictive maintenance in infrastructure. Rather than waiting for a critical failure to occur, AI algorithms can predict when a particular part of the infrastructure—such as a water pipe or power line—is likely to fail, enabling the city to carry out maintenance before an issue arises. This reduces costs, increases reliability, and prevents disruptions.

Cloud Computing and Big Data

The large volume of data generated by IoT devices and sensors necessitates powerful computing infrastructure. Cloud computing offers the scalability and storage capacity required to process and analyze vast amounts of data. With cloud platforms, cities can store data from thousands of sensors, run complex AI algorithms, and deliver real-time analytics without the need for costly on-premise hardware.

Big data analytics tools allow smart cities to extract value from large, unstructured data sets. This capability enables city managers to identify patterns in urban life, optimize services, and respond to citizens' needs more efficiently. Whether it's predicting traffic flows, identifying energy inefficiencies, or managing waste collection, big data provides the foundation for making informed decisions at every level of city governance.

IoT and Sensors: How They Enable Connectivity and Data Collection

The core of a smart city is the seamless connectivity between devices, sensors, and systems. The Internet of Things (IoT) allows cities to create a network of interconnected objects that collect data in real-time and communicate that data to centralized systems for analysis and action.

The IoT Architecture in Smart Cities

An IoT system typically consists of several layers, each responsible for different aspects of data collection, processing, and communication. These layers include the **sensing layer**, **network layer**, and **application layer**:

1. **Sensing Layer**: This layer consists of the physical sensors and devices that gather data from the environment. These sensors could include temperature sensors, humidity monitors, GPS devices, and air quality sensors. Each sensor captures specific data points that are relevant to the city's infrastructure and services.

2. **Network Layer**: Once the data is collected, it needs to be transmitted to a centralized platform for processing. The network layer ensures that the data is transmitted securely and efficiently using technologies like Wi-Fi, Bluetooth, 5G, or LPWAN (Low Power Wide Area Networks).

3. **Application Layer**: The application layer is where the data is analyzed and used to make decisions. Data from various sensors is fed into cloud-based platforms, where it is processed by AI algorithms and data analytics tools. The insights generated are used to control various systems, optimize services, and make decisions about city management.

Real-Time Data Collection with IoT Sensors

One of the primary benefits of IoT sensors is their ability to collect real-time data. In traditional cities, data collection often happens at fixed intervals or only when a problem occurs. In smart cities, data is continuously collected and analyzed, allowing for immediate responses to emerging issues. For example, IoT sensors in water pipes can detect leaks and send real-time alerts to maintenance crews before a major water outage occurs.

The Role of AI in Analyzing IoT Data

AI plays a crucial role in processing and interpreting the vast amounts of data collected by IoT sensors. Machine learning algorithms can identify patterns in the data, predict future trends, and automate decision-making processes. For instance, AI can analyze traffic sensor data to predict congestion, optimize traffic light timing, or even reroute traffic in real-time.

Hands-on Project: Setting Up an IoT Sensor to Collect Real-Time Data

In this hands-on project, we will guide you through setting up a basic IoT sensor system to collect real-time data and send it to a cloud platform for analysis. This project will give you a practical understanding of how IoT sensors work and how they contribute to building smart city systems.

Step 1: Choosing Your IoT Sensor

For this project, we will use a simple temperature and humidity sensor (such as the DHT11 or DHT22 sensor) connected to a microcontroller like the Raspberry Pi or Arduino. This sensor will collect data on the temperature and humidity levels in a room or outdoor environment.

Step 2: Connecting the Sensor to Your Microcontroller

Connect the sensor to the microcontroller following the manufacturer's instructions. For a Raspberry Pi, you will typically connect the sensor to the GPIO pins, while for an Arduino, you will use the analog or digital pins depending on the sensor model.

Step 3: Writing the Code to Collect Data

Once your sensor is connected, write a simple script in Python (for Raspberry Pi) or C++ (for Arduino) to read the data from the sensor. This script will continuously monitor the temperature and humidity levels and log the data.

Step 4: Sending the Data to the Cloud

Next, we will send the collected data to a cloud platform, such as ThingSpeak or AWS IoT. This allows you to store the data remotely and visualize it in real-time. For this, you will need to set up an account with your chosen cloud service, obtain the necessary API keys, and write a script to send data over Wi-Fi.

Step 5: Visualizing the Data

Once your data is being sent to the cloud, you can use the cloud platform's dashboard to create graphs and visualizations of the data. This will help you see trends over time, such as how the temperature or humidity levels change throughout the day.

Chapter 3: Understanding Data Analytics in Smart Cities

The backbone of a successful smart city lies not just in the integration of technologies like AI and IoT, but in how data is collected, processed, and leveraged. Data analytics plays a central role in enabling smart cities to function efficiently, make informed decisions, and continuously improve the lives of urban residents. In this chapter, we will explore the types of data collected in smart cities, how data analytics helps optimize essential city services such as traffic management, energy distribution, and waste collection, and the platforms and tools available to manage and process this data. We will also guide you through a hands-on project involving the analysis of public transportation data to optimize routes, demonstrating the practical application of data analytics in urban systems.

1. Types of Data in Smart Cities: Big Data, Real-Time Data, and Predictive Analytics

Data in smart cities can be divided into three main categories: **big data**, **real-time data**, and **predictive analytics**. Each of these types of data has its own role in optimizing city services, improving efficiency, and ensuring the sustainable development of urban environments.

Big Data in Smart Cities

Big data refers to the vast volumes of structured and unstructured data collected from multiple sources within the city. This data comes from IoT sensors, public records, social media, citizen feedback, and more. Big data is defined not just by the sheer amount of data, but also by its variety, velocity, and veracity—the "4 Vs" that characterize big data.

- **Volume**: Smart cities generate massive amounts of data daily. From traffic cameras to weather sensors, social media feeds to utility meters, every aspect of urban life produces data. This is where big data technologies come in, enabling the collection, storage, and analysis of such vast quantities.

- **Variety**: The data in smart cities is not all the same type. It can range from structured data like traffic counts or energy consumption to unstructured data like video footage or social media posts. A smart city must be able to handle this diverse mix of data.

- **Velocity**: Smart cities operate in real time, and the data they generate is often time-sensitive. Smart transportation systems, for example, rely on near-instantaneous data to adjust traffic flow, while environmental monitoring systems must track real-time changes in pollution levels.

- **Veracity**: For data to be useful, it must be accurate and reliable. Ensuring the integrity of big data is a key challenge in smart city analytics, as errors or inconsistencies in the data can lead to incorrect decisions or system failures.

Smart cities leverage big data analytics to provide better services, predict future demands, and optimize resource use. For example, analyzing historical traffic data can help predict traffic patterns, while energy consumption data can be used to optimize energy grids, reduce waste, and promote sustainability.

Real-Time Data in Smart Cities

Real-time data is the lifeblood of a smart city. It is continuously collected from various sensors, devices, and systems throughout the city. Real-time data allows cities to monitor and respond to dynamic changes in urban environments, ensuring that systems remain optimized and that interventions can be made swiftly.

- **Traffic Management**: Traffic sensors, GPS devices, and cameras provide real-time data on traffic flow, accidents, and road conditions. This data enables the city's traffic management systems to adjust light timings, provide detour routes, and even notify citizens of incidents as they occur.

- **Environmental Monitoring**: Air quality sensors provide data on pollution levels, enabling city officials to monitor the health of the environment. Similarly, weather stations collect data on temperature, humidity, and rainfall, allowing cities to prepare for extreme weather events like storms or heatwaves.

- **Public Services**: Real-time data can be used to track the performance of public services like waste management and water distribution. For example, smart waste bins equipped with sensors can alert waste management services when they are full, enabling more efficient collection.

The key advantage of real-time data is its ability to trigger immediate actions. If a sensor detects a malfunction or anomaly, the relevant systems can immediately respond, preventing problems before they escalate.

Predictive Analytics in Smart Cities

Predictive analytics is the use of historical data, statistical algorithms, and machine learning to forecast future outcomes. By analyzing past trends and identifying patterns, predictive analytics can help city officials anticipate problems and make proactive decisions.

- **Traffic Prediction**: By analyzing past traffic data, predictive models can forecast traffic congestion during peak hours or special events. This allows for dynamic adjustments to traffic flow, such as altering traffic signal timings or suggesting alternative routes to commuters.

- **Energy Demand Forecasting**: Predictive models can forecast energy consumption patterns based on historical data and external factors like weather conditions. This allows cities to adjust the energy grid in anticipation of high demand, reducing the risk of power outages and ensuring that energy resources are distributed efficiently.

- **Public Health and Safety**: Predictive analytics can also be used to identify potential health outbreaks by monitoring trends in disease reporting or social media activity. By detecting patterns in real time, cities can take preventive measures before an outbreak becomes widespread.

Predictive analytics empowers cities to act before problems arise, reducing the need for reactive measures and optimizing resource allocation.

2. How Data Analytics Helps Optimize City Services: Traffic, Energy, and Waste Management

Data analytics is revolutionizing the way cities manage essential services like transportation, energy, and waste management. By harnessing the power of data, smart cities can optimize these systems to run more efficiently, reduce costs, and improve sustainability.

Traffic Optimization

One of the most critical applications of data analytics in smart cities is traffic management. Cities face significant traffic congestion, pollution, and inefficiency, all of which can be mitigated with the right data-driven systems.

- **Traffic Flow Optimization**: Data from traffic sensors, GPS devices, and cameras can be analyzed in real time to optimize traffic light timings, adjust lanes, and manage congestion. AI and machine learning algorithms can predict when certain areas will experience heavy traffic and adjust the traffic signals accordingly.

- **Congestion Pricing**: By analyzing traffic patterns, cities can implement congestion pricing systems that charge higher fees during peak hours, encouraging drivers to travel during off-peak times or use public transport.

- **Smart Parking**: IoT-enabled parking systems provide real-time information about available parking spaces. Data analytics helps drivers find the nearest available spots, reducing the time spent circling for parking, which in turn reduces traffic and emissions.

Energy Management

Cities consume vast amounts of energy, and managing this consumption is critical for reducing costs and promoting sustainability. Data analytics allows cities to optimize energy use by analyzing consumption patterns and forecasting demand.

- **Smart Grids**: A smart grid is an electrical grid that uses data analytics and IoT technology to monitor and manage the flow of electricity. Smart meters allow for real-time monitoring of energy consumption, while predictive analytics help forecast demand and adjust the grid accordingly.

- **Renewable Energy Integration**: Data analytics can be used to integrate renewable energy sources like solar and wind into the grid. By forecasting weather conditions and energy production from renewable sources, cities can optimize energy distribution and reduce reliance on non-renewable sources.

- **Energy Efficiency**: By analyzing data from smart buildings and homes, cities can identify areas of high energy consumption and take action to reduce waste. For example, buildings can automatically adjust their HVAC systems based on occupancy or weather conditions.

Waste Management

Waste management is another area where data analytics plays a transformative role. Traditional waste management systems are often inefficient, with waste collection based on fixed schedules rather than real-time need. Smart waste management systems use data to improve efficiency, reduce costs, and promote sustainability.

- **Smart Bins**: IoT-enabled waste bins equipped with sensors can detect when they are full and send alerts to waste management services. This ensures that waste is collected on time, preventing overflowing bins and reducing unnecessary collection trips.

- **Route Optimization**: Data analytics is used to optimize waste collection routes, reducing fuel consumption and carbon emissions. By analyzing data on traffic patterns, waste levels, and vehicle performance, waste management services can create the most efficient routes for their fleet.

- **Recycling Optimization**: Data analytics can help improve recycling efforts by identifying which areas are underperforming in terms of recycling rates. By analyzing waste composition, cities can develop targeted campaigns to encourage better recycling practices and reduce landfill waste.

3. Tools and Platforms for Data Analytics in Smart Cities

As cities accumulate vast amounts of data, managing and analyzing it becomes increasingly complex. Fortunately, there are numerous tools and platforms that make it easier to store, process, and analyze the data collected from various sources.

Cloud Computing and Big Data Platforms

Cloud computing is an essential tool for managing big data in smart cities. Cloud platforms offer scalable storage, computing power, and analytics capabilities that allow cities to handle vast amounts of data without the need for on-premise infrastructure. Popular cloud platforms for smart cities include:

- **Amazon Web Services (AWS)**: AWS offers a range of tools for big data analytics, including data lakes, machine learning, and real-time data processing services.

- **Microsoft Azure**: Azure provides cloud-based solutions for data storage, analytics, and AI, helping cities analyze data at scale and make data-driven decisions.

- **Google Cloud**: Google Cloud offers tools like BigQuery for data analysis, TensorFlow for machine learning, and Cloud IoT for managing IoT devices, making it ideal for smart city applications.

Data Analytics and Visualization Tools

Once data is collected and stored, it needs to be processed and analyzed. Data analytics platforms help city officials interpret data and extract meaningful insights. Some of the most widely used platforms include:

- **Tableau**: Tableau is a powerful data visualization tool that allows cities to create interactive dashboards and visualizations of their data. It's widely used for presenting data to stakeholders and decision-makers in an easily digestible format.

- **Power BI**: Power BI, from Microsoft, is another popular data visualization and business intelligence tool. It integrates well with other Microsoft services, making it an ideal choice for many organizations.

- **QlikView**: QlikView offers a comprehensive suite of analytics tools, including dashboards, reports, and predictive analytics, enabling cities to visualize data and uncover insights.

Machine Learning and AI Platforms

Machine learning and AI are essential for predictive analytics in smart cities. These technologies help cities analyze historical data, predict future trends, and automate decision-making. Popular AI platforms include:

- **TensorFlow**: Developed by Google, TensorFlow is an open-source machine learning framework used to build predictive models for everything from traffic management to energy forecasting.

- **Apache Spark**: Apache Spark is a fast, open-source data processing engine for big data analytics. It's ideal for smart cities looking to analyze large datasets in real time.

- **H2O.ai**: H2O.ai offers open-source machine learning platforms that allow cities to build machine learning models for predictive analytics in various applications.

4. Hands-on Project: Analyzing Public Transportation Data to Optimize Routes

In this hands-on project, we will work with real-world public transportation data to optimize bus routes using data analytics. This project will demonstrate how to use historical data to make predictions and improve the efficiency of public transit systems.

Step 1: Obtain Public Transportation Data

The first step in our project is to obtain public transportation data. Many cities provide open data portals with datasets on bus routes, stop locations, and travel times. These datasets are often available in CSV or JSON format.

Step 2: Load and Clean the Data

Once you have the data, load it into a data analysis tool like **Pandas** in Python. Clean the data by handling missing values, removing duplicates, and ensuring the data is in a format suitable for analysis.

Step 3: Analyze Traffic and Travel Time Patterns

Using data visualization tools like **Matplotlib** or **Tableau**, create charts that show travel times for different bus routes, peak travel times, and areas with high congestion. This will help you understand patterns and identify bottlenecks in the system.

Step 4: Predictive Modeling for Route Optimization

Next, we will build a predictive model using machine learning techniques to forecast travel times based on factors like time of day, weather, and traffic conditions. Use **scikit-learn** in Python to implement regression models that predict travel times for each bus route.

Step 5: Optimize Routes

Finally, using the insights from the data analysis and predictive models, recommend optimized bus routes and schedules. This might involve adjusting route timings to avoid peak congestion, adding buses during high-demand hours, or changing routes to improve efficiency.

Chapter 4: AI in Urban Infrastructure

The rapid development of urban areas across the globe is being shaped by an innovative force that has the power to transform every aspect of urban life: Artificial Intelligence (AI). From city planning and development to infrastructure maintenance, energy management, and resource allocation, AI is playing a pivotal role in making cities smarter, more efficient, and more sustainable. As the heart of the smart city, urban infrastructure is undergoing a digital transformation powered by AI, which is enabling cities to meet the challenges of rapid urbanization, environmental sustainability, and rising expectations from urban dwellers.

In this chapter, we will explore how AI is transforming urban infrastructure, delving into its applications in city planning and development, predictive maintenance of infrastructure, and energy management. By the end of this chapter, you will have a solid understanding of how AI is reshaping the built environment, from smarter buildings and streets to fully integrated city-wide systems. We will also guide you through a hands-on project where you'll design an AI system for smart grid management—one of the most crucial components of a modern smart city.

1. AI in City Planning and Development

City planning is no longer just about creating functional spaces for living, working, and commuting; it's about creating an environment that is efficient, sustainable, and adaptable to future needs. AI is revolutionizing the way cities are planned, designed, and developed, allowing urban planners and developers to harness vast amounts of data, make informed decisions, and optimize designs for better quality of life.

Data-Driven Urban Planning

AI's role in urban planning begins with the collection and analysis of massive datasets, often referred to as "big data." These datasets include information from a variety of sources: satellite imagery, traffic sensors, utility meters, weather data, social media feeds, and more. The challenge for urban planners is not just collecting this data but interpreting it to inform decisions on zoning, infrastructure development, and resource management.

AI-powered data analytics tools help planners analyze historical trends and project future needs. For example, AI algorithms can process traffic flow data to predict congestion points, helping to design transportation networks that minimize bottlenecks. Similarly, data from public health records, air quality sensors, and social media activity can be analyzed to identify areas with high pollution levels or inadequate healthcare access, enabling targeted urban interventions.

Example: AI-Optimized Urban Zoning
AI systems can optimize urban zoning by analyzing land use patterns and predicting how different areas of a city will develop. Using machine learning, AI models can predict the best locations for residential, commercial, and industrial zones based on population growth, economic trends, and environmental factors. By identifying high-potential zones, city planners can make data-driven decisions on where to place critical infrastructure like schools, hospitals, and transportation hubs.

Smart Mobility and Transport Systems

Urban transport systems are some of the most critical aspects of city planning, and AI is driving major improvements in this area. Smart cities are leveraging AI to design and implement integrated transport systems that can improve traffic flow, reduce congestion, and provide alternative transportation options.

- **AI-Powered Traffic Flow Management**: AI algorithms are used to monitor and manage traffic flow in real-time. Cameras and sensors placed at intersections provide data on traffic volume, vehicle speed, and congestion levels. AI models process this data to optimize traffic signal timings, manage traffic density, and provide real-time updates to drivers. In cities like Los Angeles, AI-powered traffic management systems have reduced congestion and improved air quality by dynamically adjusting signal timings based on real-time traffic conditions.

- **Autonomous Vehicles and Public Transport**: Autonomous vehicles (AVs) are being integrated into the transport landscape of smart cities. AI is responsible for the development of AV systems, enabling them to interact with traffic, pedestrians, and other vehicles. In addition, AI is being used to optimize public transport systems by predicting demand, adjusting schedules, and ensuring that routes are efficient and cost-effective.

Building Resilience and Sustainability

Urban development is increasingly focused on sustainability, and AI plays a crucial role in ensuring that cities can meet environmental goals. AI is used to monitor resource consumption, reduce waste, and promote sustainability across various sectors.

Example: Sustainable Architecture

AI is used in sustainable architecture to design buildings that are energy-efficient, resilient to climate change, and conducive to better living conditions. Machine learning algorithms can analyze weather patterns, building materials, and environmental factors to create energy-efficient designs that minimize resource consumption. For example, AI can simulate how different building materials will perform under various climate conditions, helping architects select the best options for energy efficiency and durability.

2. Predictive Maintenance of Infrastructure

One of the most significant applications of AI in urban infrastructure is predictive maintenance. Traditional infrastructure management often involves reactive measures, such as waiting for a problem to occur before addressing it. Predictive maintenance, powered by AI, allows cities to take a proactive approach, identifying potential failures before they happen and addressing them before they cause significant disruption.

Sensors and IoT in Predictive Maintenance

In smart cities, IoT devices and sensors are embedded in various pieces of infrastructure, including roads, bridges, tunnels, water pipes, and electrical grids. These sensors collect real-time data on the health and performance of infrastructure, such as temperature, vibration, pressure, and humidity levels. AI algorithms process this data to detect anomalies and predict when maintenance will be needed.

For example, in bridge maintenance, AI-powered systems can monitor the structural integrity of a bridge by analyzing vibration patterns. If the system detects unusual vibrations, it may signal that a particular component of the bridge is at risk of failure, prompting an inspection or repair before the problem escalates into a safety hazard.

Optimizing Maintenance Schedules

Predictive maintenance can help cities optimize their maintenance schedules by prioritizing repairs based on real-time data. AI can predict when components will fail and prioritize resources accordingly. For example, AI models can predict when a water pipe is likely to burst based on factors like age, material, pressure fluctuations, and historical data. This allows the city to replace or repair pipes before they fail, preventing costly water outages and minimizing disruption to residents.

Example: AI in Railway Infrastructure

AI is widely used in rail systems for predictive maintenance. By collecting data from sensors embedded in the railway tracks, trains, and stations, AI models can monitor the health of the railway infrastructure in real-time. These models can predict issues such as track wear, equipment malfunctions, and signal failures. By proactively addressing maintenance needs, rail systems can reduce downtime, improve safety, and lower operating costs.

Real-World Case Study: Predictive Maintenance in London

London's Crossrail project uses AI-powered predictive maintenance to monitor the condition of tunnels, tracks, and other infrastructure. Using a combination of IoT sensors and machine learning algorithms, the system can detect wear and tear, identify potential hazards, and optimize maintenance schedules. The project has been successful in reducing downtime and improving the overall reliability of the rail network.

3. AI for Energy Management and Resource Allocation

Energy management and resource allocation are fundamental challenges for modern cities. Cities are increasingly turning to AI to optimize the consumption of resources, reduce waste, and ensure that energy is distributed efficiently. With growing concerns about climate change and sustainability, AI is playing a vital role in creating more energy-efficient, resilient, and sustainable cities.

AI in Smart Grid Management

One of the most significant AI applications in energy management is the smart grid. A smart grid is an electrical grid that uses digital communication technology to detect and react to local changes in electricity usage. It is designed to enhance the efficiency, reliability, and sustainability of electricity distribution. AI is used to analyze real-time data from smart meters, sensors, and power plants, making the grid more responsive to changes in energy demand.

- **Energy Demand Forecasting**: AI can forecast energy demand by analyzing historical consumption data and external factors like weather, time of day, and seasonality. Machine learning models help predict peak demand periods, enabling utilities to adjust energy distribution proactively and avoid overloads.

- **Renewable Energy Integration**: Smart grids also incorporate renewable energy sources, such as solar and wind power. However, renewable energy production is often intermittent, with fluctuations depending on weather conditions. AI helps balance the supply and demand of energy by forecasting renewable energy production and adjusting the grid accordingly. This enables the integration of renewable energy sources without compromising grid stability.

Smart Building Energy Management

AI is also used in smart buildings to optimize energy usage. Building management systems (BMS) are responsible for controlling the heating, ventilation, air conditioning (HVAC), lighting, and other energy-consuming systems in a building. AI is integrated into these systems to reduce energy waste and improve efficiency.

- **Dynamic Temperature and Lighting Control**: AI algorithms can learn the occupancy patterns in a building and adjust heating, lighting, and cooling systems accordingly. For example, AI can reduce the HVAC load in unoccupied rooms, ensuring that energy is only used where it's needed.

- **Predictive Maintenance for HVAC Systems**: Similar to predictive maintenance for infrastructure, AI can also monitor the performance of HVAC systems in buildings. By analyzing historical data on temperature, humidity, and airflow, AI models can predict when maintenance or repairs are required, preventing system failures and ensuring optimal energy efficiency.

Example: AI-Powered Energy Management in Smart Cities

In cities like San Diego, AI-powered energy management systems are used to balance energy supply and demand, optimize the use of renewable energy, and reduce energy waste. The system can analyze data from sensors in buildings, streetlights, and utility meters to optimize energy distribution in real-time, ensuring that the city's energy consumption remains efficient and sustainable.

Smart Water Management

In addition to energy, AI is increasingly being used in smart water management systems to ensure efficient use of water resources. AI models can analyze real-time data from water meters, sensors, and weather forecasts to predict water demand and optimize distribution.

- **Water Leak Detection**: AI can detect leaks in water pipes by analyzing pressure data from sensors. The system can alert maintenance teams when a leak is detected, reducing water loss and preventing costly repairs.

- **Irrigation Control**: AI models can optimize irrigation systems by predicting weather patterns and adjusting water distribution accordingly. For example, if heavy rainfall is forecasted, the system can reduce water usage in agricultural or urban landscapes, preventing water waste.

4. Hands-on Project: Designing an AI System for Smart Grid Management

Now that we've explored the role of AI in urban infrastructure, let's dive into a practical application. In this hands-on project, we will design an AI system for smart grid management. The goal is to create a system that can optimize energy distribution, forecast demand, and integrate renewable energy sources.

Step 1: Define the Problem and Set Up the Data Pipeline

To begin, we will define the key components of the smart grid: energy consumption, energy generation (from renewable sources), weather data, and historical energy usage. Using data from smart meters, IoT sensors, and weather APIs, we will set up a data pipeline that collects and processes the relevant data in real-time.

Step 2: Build the AI Model for Demand Forecasting

Using machine learning techniques like regression analysis or time series forecasting, we will build a predictive model that can forecast energy demand. The model will be trained on historical data, such as hourly energy consumption, temperature, and weather conditions, to predict future demand for energy in the smart grid.

Step 3: Implement Real-Time Data Integration

Once the predictive model is built, we will implement real-time data integration. This involves connecting the AI system to live data from smart meters, IoT sensors, and weather forecasts. The system will continuously update its predictions and adjust the grid's energy distribution accordingly.

Step 4: Optimize Energy Distribution

The AI system will use its demand forecasting capabilities to optimize energy distribution across the grid. By analyzing real-time data on energy production from renewable sources, the system will adjust energy allocation to ensure that the grid remains stable and energy-efficient.

Step 5: Evaluate and Test the System

Finally, we will test the AI system by evaluating its performance using historical data. The goal is to ensure that the system can predict energy demand accurately, optimize distribution, and integrate renewable energy sources without causing grid instability.

Chapter 5: The Role of IoT in Smart Cities

The Internet of Things (IoT) stands as one of the foundational technologies driving the transformation of cities around the globe into "smart cities." By embedding everyday objects with sensors, communication devices, and smart capabilities, IoT creates a network of interconnected systems that enables cities to operate more efficiently, sustainably, and safely. Whether it's optimizing traffic flow, managing energy consumption, or enhancing healthcare services, IoT plays a central role in shaping the future of urban living.

In this chapter, we will explore how IoT functions as the backbone of a smart city. We will delve into the IoT networks and devices that are used to gather and transmit data, the specific roles IoT plays in smart city initiatives like smart homes, transportation, and healthcare, and the communication protocols that make IoT systems interoperable. Additionally, we will walk through a hands-on project where you will build a basic IoT-enabled smart home system, giving you the tools to create your own smart solutions.

1. IoT Networks and Devices: Sensors, Actuators, and Connectivity

At its core, IoT is a system of devices that are connected to the internet and capable of communicating with each other. These devices can include anything from streetlights and traffic sensors to smart refrigerators and medical monitoring equipment. To understand how IoT functions in smart cities, it's important to first understand the various components that make up an IoT system.

Sensors: The Eyes and Ears of IoT

Sensors are the critical input devices in any IoT system. These small devices collect data from the environment and convert it into signals that can be transmitted over a network. There are many types of sensors used in smart cities, each designed to gather specific kinds of data, such as temperature, humidity, light, pressure, motion, and more.

- **Traffic Sensors**: IoT-based traffic sensors detect vehicle movement, congestion, and speed. By analyzing this data, cities can optimize traffic flow and reduce congestion.

- **Environmental Sensors**: These sensors monitor air quality, pollution levels, temperature, and humidity, helping cities stay on top of environmental health and respond proactively to pollution spikes.

- **Smart Meters**: IoT-enabled smart meters monitor energy, water, and gas consumption in real-time. This data allows utilities to optimize usage, reduce waste, and improve resource allocation.

The primary purpose of these sensors is to gather raw data from the environment, which will later be processed and analyzed to gain insights for various applications within a smart city.

Actuators: The Hands of IoT

While sensors collect data, actuators act upon that data to bring about physical change in the environment. Actuators are devices that respond to commands from a central control system, often performing mechanical actions based on sensor data. For example, actuators in traffic management systems may adjust traffic lights or gates based on real-time data collected from traffic sensors.

- **Smart Streetlights**: Actuators in streetlights can adjust brightness based on the time of day or surrounding conditions, or they can turn off completely when no movement is detected.

- **HVAC Systems**: In smart buildings or homes, actuators control heating, ventilation, and air conditioning (HVAC) systems, adjusting the temperature based on real-time data from temperature sensors and user preferences.

By acting on sensor data, actuators allow IoT systems to automate processes and make cities more responsive and adaptive.

Connectivity: The Nervous System of IoT

The connectivity layer is what allows IoT devices to communicate with each other and with a central system. Without robust connectivity, the IoT system would be disjointed and inefficient. There are multiple connectivity options available, including:

- **Wi-Fi**: Widely used in urban environments, Wi-Fi allows devices to communicate over relatively short distances and is ideal for use in homes and buildings.

- **Bluetooth**: This short-range communication protocol is used in applications like smart locks, health devices, and personal area networks (PANs).

- **Cellular Networks**: For devices that require wide-area communication, cellular networks like 4G, 5G, and Narrowband IoT (NB-IoT) provide a reliable and scalable solution.

- **LPWAN (Low Power Wide Area Networks)**: Technologies like LoRaWAN and Sigfox provide low-power, long-range communication that is ideal for IoT applications such as smart agriculture, asset tracking, and environmental monitoring.

The choice of connectivity technology depends on the application. Smart homes and buildings typically use Wi-Fi, while outdoor sensors may rely on LoRaWAN for long-range communication without draining battery life.

2. How IoT Supports Smart City Initiatives

IoT's true potential lies in its ability to enable smart city initiatives. Whether it's making a home more energy-efficient, improving public transportation systems, or optimizing healthcare services, IoT is the driving force behind the innovative solutions that are reshaping urban environments.

Smart Homes

A smart home is a living space equipped with IoT devices that can be controlled remotely, automated, and integrated into a larger smart city ecosystem. IoT-enabled homes are more energy-efficient, secure, and convenient, offering significant benefits to residents.

- **Energy Management**: IoT devices such as smart thermostats, smart lights, and energy meters allow homeowners to monitor and control energy usage remotely. These devices can automatically adjust settings based on occupancy or time of day, reducing energy consumption and costs.

- **Security**: IoT-based security systems, such as smart locks, cameras, and motion detectors, provide enhanced protection for homes. Residents can monitor their property remotely and receive alerts in case of unusual activity.

- **Automation**: IoT systems can automate routine tasks, such as turning lights on when someone enters a room, adjusting the thermostat when the temperature changes, or even feeding pets at specific times.

Example: Smart Home Integration with Smart Cities

In cities like Barcelona, smart homes are integrated into the larger smart city ecosystem. For example, residents can use a city-wide platform to control not only their home but also interact with public services such as public transportation, garbage collection, and energy usage. By linking homes with city infrastructure, IoT helps improve both the efficiency and sustainability of the entire urban environment.

Smart Transportation

IoT enables smarter, more efficient transportation systems by providing real-time data that helps optimize routes, improve safety, and reduce congestion.

- **Intelligent Traffic Management**: IoT-based sensors monitor traffic conditions and send real-time data to a central traffic management system. This system can adjust traffic lights to minimize congestion, control traffic flow, and even predict traffic patterns for future planning.

- **Smart Parking**: IoT sensors in parking spaces detect when a spot is occupied and communicate this information to drivers via mobile apps. This reduces the time spent searching for parking and helps reduce traffic congestion.

- **Autonomous Vehicles**: IoT plays a key role in the development of self-driving cars. By providing real-time communication between vehicles, sensors, and infrastructure, IoT enables autonomous vehicles to navigate cities safely and efficiently.

Example: Singapore's Smart Traffic System

Singapore has implemented an intelligent traffic management system that uses IoT to monitor and control traffic flow across the city. Sensors embedded in roads collect real-time data on traffic congestion, and AI algorithms process this data to adjust traffic lights, manage traffic lanes, and notify drivers of accidents or delays. This system has been crucial in reducing congestion and improving the overall efficiency of the transportation network.

Smart Healthcare

Healthcare is one of the most critical sectors benefiting from IoT in smart cities. IoT enables the development of systems that improve patient care, reduce costs, and enhance the efficiency of healthcare services.

- **Remote Monitoring**: IoT-enabled wearable devices, such as smartwatches and health trackers, continuously monitor a patient's vital signs, such as heart rate, blood pressure, and glucose levels. This data can be sent to healthcare providers in real-time, allowing for remote monitoring and early detection of health issues.

- **Smart Hospitals**: IoT devices are used in hospitals to track medical equipment, monitor patient status, and ensure that resources are allocated efficiently. For example, RFID tags can track hospital beds, surgical tools, and medications, ensuring they are available when needed.

- **Telemedicine**: IoT enables telemedicine solutions that allow patients to receive healthcare services remotely, either through video consultations or remote diagnostic tools.

Example: AI-Driven Healthcare Systems

IoT devices in healthcare are often integrated with AI algorithms to enhance decision-making. In some smart cities, data from medical devices is analyzed by AI systems to detect patterns that may indicate the onset of a disease. For example, AI can analyze data from wearable ECG monitors to detect early signs of heart failure, allowing for timely intervention.

3. IoT Communication Protocols: MQTT, Zigbee, LoRaWAN

For IoT systems to function properly, they require reliable communication protocols that ensure devices can exchange data efficiently and securely. Several communication protocols are used in smart cities, each with its own advantages depending on the application.

MQTT (Message Queuing Telemetry Transport)

MQTT is a lightweight messaging protocol that is commonly used in IoT applications. It is designed to be simple and efficient, requiring minimal bandwidth and providing real-time data transfer.

- **Use Cases**: MQTT is ideal for applications that require real-time communication, such as home automation, smart buildings, and energy management systems.

- **Advantages**: Its low power consumption and small code footprint make it ideal for IoT devices with limited resources.

- **How it Works**: MQTT works on a publisher-subscriber model, where devices (publishers) send data to a central server (broker), and other devices (subscribers) can receive the data as needed.

Zigbee

Zigbee is a low-power, low-data-rate wireless communication protocol designed for short-range communication in IoT networks. It is commonly used in home automation and industrial applications.

- **Use Cases**: Zigbee is widely used in smart homes for devices like light bulbs, smart locks, and temperature sensors. It is also used in industrial IoT (IIoT) for monitoring and controlling equipment.

- **Advantages**: Zigbee supports mesh networking, which allows devices to communicate with each other directly, improving range and reliability.

- **How it Works**: Devices in a Zigbee network form a mesh, with each device acting as both a transmitter and receiver, passing messages along to other devices to extend the network.

LoRaWAN (Long Range Wide Area Network)

LoRaWAN is a long-range, low-power communication protocol designed for wide-area IoT applications. It is particularly useful for IoT systems that require devices to communicate over large distances while using minimal energy.

- **Use Cases**: LoRaWAN is ideal for smart city applications such as environmental monitoring, smart agriculture, and asset tracking.

- **Advantages**: LoRaWAN can transmit data over long distances (up to 15 km in urban environments) while consuming very little power, making it suitable for battery-operated sensors.

- **How it Works**: LoRaWAN uses low-power wide-area networks (LPWANs) to send small packets of data over long distances. It is designed for devices that only need to send small amounts of data intermittently, such as environmental sensors.

4. Hands-On Project: Building a Basic IoT-Enabled Smart Home System

In this hands-on project, you will build a basic IoT-enabled smart home system using popular devices and sensors. The system will allow you to control lights and monitor temperature remotely, simulating the experience of living in a smart home.

Step 1: Choose the Devices and Components

For this project, you will need:

- **Raspberry Pi** or **Arduino** microcontroller

- **Temperature sensor** (e.g., DHT11)

- **Smart light bulbs** (e.g., Philips Hue)

- **Relay module** (for controlling appliances)

- **Wi-Fi module** (e.g., ESP8266 for Arduino or built-in Wi-Fi on Raspberry Pi)

- **Cloud platform** (e.g., ThingSpeak or Blynk)

Step 2: Set Up the Microcontroller

Begin by setting up the Raspberry Pi or Arduino and connecting it to your Wi-Fi network. You will also need to install the necessary libraries for the sensors and actuators.

Step 3: Integrate the Sensors and Actuators

Connect the temperature sensor to the microcontroller and the smart lights or relay module to the system. The temperature sensor will collect data, which will be displayed on a cloud dashboard, while the smart light bulb will be controlled based on predefined conditions (such as turning on when motion is detected).

Step 4: Create a Cloud Dashboard

Create a dashboard on a cloud platform like ThingSpeak or Blynk, where you can monitor the temperature and control the smart light bulb remotely.

Step 5: Program the System

Write a script to read the data from the temperature sensor and send it to the cloud. Additionally, write a script to control the light based on specific conditions, such as turning it on when the temperature exceeds a certain threshold.

Step 6: Test the System

Once the system is set up and running, test it by monitoring the temperature remotely and controlling the lights based on the readings. Make adjustments as needed to refine the system.

Chapter 6: Smart Traffic Systems and AI

Urban transportation systems are a vital component of any modern city, and with the increasing complexity of urban mobility, managing traffic has become one of the most pressing challenges for urban planners. From congestion and accidents to environmental concerns, traditional traffic management systems often fall short in optimizing the flow of traffic, reducing emissions, and enhancing safety. Enter AI-powered smart traffic systems—these systems use artificial intelligence (AI), machine learning (ML), and real-time data to provide intelligent, adaptive solutions that make traffic management more efficient, safer, and environmentally friendly.

In this chapter, we will explore how AI is transforming traffic systems in smart cities. From AI-powered traffic lights and smart intersections to machine learning for traffic prediction and congestion management, we will cover the technologies and techniques behind smart traffic solutions. We will also walk through a hands-on project where you will build a simple AI-based traffic light controller, giving you the tools to understand how AI can improve traffic management and efficiency.

1. AI-Powered Traffic Lights and Smart Intersections

One of the most visible applications of AI in traffic management is the AI-powered traffic light system. Unlike traditional traffic lights, which operate on fixed timers or simple sensors, AI-powered traffic lights are dynamic, responding in real-time to traffic flow, congestion, and even accidents. These intelligent systems optimize traffic light timing to reduce congestion, improve traffic flow, and reduce fuel consumption and emissions.

AI-Driven Traffic Light Systems

Traditional traffic lights are programmed with fixed schedules or reactive systems that adjust signal timings based on vehicle counts or preset rules. While this system works to an extent, it does not respond efficiently to changes in traffic conditions, such as traffic jams, accidents, or events like concerts or sporting events, which can drastically alter traffic patterns. AI-powered traffic light systems address this problem by using machine learning algorithms to adjust traffic light timings based on real-time data.

How AI-Powered Traffic Lights Work:

1. **Real-Time Data Collection**: Cameras and sensors placed at intersections gather real-time data on traffic flow, including the number of vehicles, their speed, and even pedestrian activity.

2. **Data Analysis with AI**: The collected data is fed into machine learning algorithms, which analyze the current traffic conditions. The AI system then adjusts the traffic light timings based on the data, giving priority to congested lanes or making real-time adjustments to accommodate unforeseen delays.

3. **Adaptive Signal Control**: AI systems can adapt to dynamic traffic patterns, optimizing the flow of traffic during peak hours, reducing congestion, and improving overall traffic

management. For example, if a lane is heavily congested, the system can extend the green light for that lane and shorten the green light for lanes with less traffic.

Example: Optimizing Intersections with AI

Cities like Los Angeles, San Francisco, and Singapore are already experimenting with AI-powered traffic light systems. In Los Angeles, the city has implemented a system called the Adaptive Traffic Signal System (ATSAC), which uses real-time traffic data to adjust signal timings dynamically. This system has led to a reduction in traffic delays and improved the overall efficiency of the city's transportation network.

Smart Intersections

Smart intersections take AI-powered traffic management a step further. These intersections use advanced sensors, cameras, and AI algorithms to monitor and manage the flow of traffic. Unlike traditional intersections, which rely solely on fixed signals, smart intersections can provide real-time updates and respond dynamically to changing conditions.

Key Features of Smart Intersections:

1. **Real-Time Communication**: Smart intersections communicate with other smart city systems, such as public transportation and emergency response vehicles, to prioritize traffic and optimize flow.

2. **Vehicle-to-Infrastructure (V2I) Communication**: Smart intersections can communicate directly with connected vehicles (CVs) to optimize signal timings and avoid collisions. For example, if a connected vehicle is approaching a red light, the system can adjust the signal to allow the vehicle to pass through more smoothly, reducing delays.

3. **Pedestrian and Cyclist Integration**: Smart intersections can also account for pedestrian and cyclist traffic. Using sensors to detect pedestrians waiting to cross, the system can adjust light cycles to minimize wait times, improving the safety and accessibility of the intersection.

Example: Smart Intersection in Columbus, Ohio
Columbus, Ohio, implemented an innovative smart

intersection project that integrates traffic signals, public transit, and connected vehicles. The system uses real-time data to optimize traffic flow and reduce congestion, resulting in improved travel times and increased safety for all road users.

2. Using Machine Learning for Traffic Prediction and Congestion Management

Machine learning, a subset of AI, plays a pivotal role in predicting traffic patterns and managing congestion. Unlike traditional methods that rely on historical traffic data, machine learning models can learn from real-time data, make predictions, and even forecast future traffic trends based on a variety of factors, such as time of day, weather conditions, and special events.

Traffic Prediction Models

Traffic prediction is the process of forecasting traffic conditions based on historical and real-time data. Machine learning models are particularly suited to this task because they can analyze large amounts of data and identify patterns that are not immediately obvious to human analysts.

Types of Traffic Prediction Models:

1. **Regression Models**: These models predict traffic flow based on historical data, such as traffic volumes, weather conditions, and road conditions. The model learns to predict future traffic patterns by analyzing past data and identifying correlations.

2. **Time Series Forecasting**: Time series forecasting techniques like ARIMA (AutoRegressive Integrated Moving Average) and LSTM (Long Short-Term Memory) networks are used to predict traffic volume at specific times of the day. These models take into account trends, seasonality, and irregular patterns to provide accurate traffic predictions.

3. **Deep Learning for Traffic Prediction**: Deep learning models, such as convolutional neural networks (CNNs) and recurrent neural networks (RNNs), are used to predict complex traffic patterns. These models can analyze spatial and temporal data from various sources, including GPS devices, traffic sensors, and even weather data, to make highly accurate predictions about traffic conditions.

Congestion Management with AI

Traffic congestion is one of the major issues in urban areas. AI and machine learning can be used to not only predict congestion but also manage it by adjusting traffic signal timings, rerouting vehicles, or providing real-time traffic updates to drivers.

Methods for AI-Powered Congestion Management:

1. **Dynamic Traffic Signal Control**: Machine learning algorithms can adjust traffic signal timings in real-time based on data from sensors and cameras. By optimizing traffic lights, the system can reduce bottlenecks, minimize delays, and enhance the flow of traffic.

2. **Intelligent Routing Systems**: AI-powered routing apps like Google Maps and Waze use real-time traffic data and machine learning to suggest the best routes for drivers, avoiding congestion and minimizing travel time. These systems learn from past data and real-time conditions to offer dynamic route recommendations.

3. **Incident Detection and Response**: AI can be used to detect traffic incidents such as

accidents or road closures by analyzing data from traffic cameras, sensors, and social media feeds. Once an incident is detected, the system can notify drivers and adjust traffic signals to clear alternative routes, reducing congestion and improving response times.

Example: Predictive Traffic Management in San Francisco

In San Francisco, the city has implemented a predictive traffic management system that uses machine learning to predict traffic congestion based on historical and real-time data. This system adjusts traffic light timings and provides drivers with real-time updates on the best routes to avoid congestion. The system has resulted in smoother traffic flow and reduced travel times for commuters.

3. Real-Time Data for Adaptive Traffic Systems

One of the most powerful features of AI-powered traffic systems is their ability to process and react to real-time data. Real-time data allows traffic systems to adjust dynamically to changes in traffic conditions, ensuring that congestion is minimized and traffic flow is optimized.

Data Sources for Real-Time Traffic Systems

AI-powered adaptive traffic systems rely on a variety of data sources to monitor traffic conditions in real-time. These include:

1. **Traffic Cameras**: Cameras placed at intersections and along roads provide visual data on traffic flow, vehicle speed, and accidents. AI algorithms can analyze this data to detect congestion and adjust traffic lights accordingly.

2. **Inductive Loop Sensors**: These sensors embedded in the road surface detect the presence of vehicles. They are commonly used to detect traffic volume and vehicle speed, feeding real-time data into the traffic management system.

3. **GPS Data**: GPS data from vehicles, taxis, ride-sharing apps, and even public transportation systems provides real-time information on traffic speed, travel times, and route choices.

This data can be used to predict congestion and optimize traffic flow.

How Real-Time Data Improves Traffic Flow

Real-time data allows AI-powered traffic systems to adjust to changes in traffic conditions immediately. This includes:

1. **Dynamic Adjustment of Traffic Lights**: Based on real-time data, AI systems can adjust the timing of traffic lights to give priority to congested lanes or adjust for traffic volume at a specific intersection.

2. **Dynamic Lane Management**: In cities with high traffic volumes, AI can dynamically manage lanes by converting general lanes into bus-only or HOV (High Occupancy Vehicle)-only lanes depending on traffic conditions. This ensures that limited resources are allocated efficiently.

3. **Incident Management**: Real-time data from sensors and cameras allows traffic systems to detect incidents such as accidents or broken-down vehicles. Once an incident is detected, AI systems can reroute traffic, adjust signal

timings, and inform drivers of alternative routes to minimize delays.

Example: Real-Time Traffic Management in Seoul

Seoul, South Korea, has developed a real-time traffic management system that uses AI and data analytics to optimize traffic flow. The system collects data from thousands of sensors across the city, which is then processed by AI algorithms to adjust traffic light timings, provide route recommendations to drivers, and manage congestion. The system has significantly reduced traffic congestion and improved air quality by minimizing idling times.

4. Hands-On Project: Building a Simple AI-Based Traffic Light Controller

In this hands-on project, we will walk through building a simple AI-based traffic light controller that dynamically adjusts the light timings based on real-time traffic data. This project will give you a practical understanding of how AI-powered traffic systems work.

Step 1: Set Up Your Hardware

To begin, you will need:

- **Raspberry Pi** or **Arduino** (we'll use a Raspberry Pi for this project)

- **LEDs** (representing traffic lights: Red, Yellow, Green)

- **PIR motion sensor** (to simulate traffic flow)

- **Resistors, jumper wires, and breadboard**

Step 2: Connect the Hardware

Connect the LEDs to the Raspberry Pi's GPIO pins to represent the traffic lights. Additionally, connect the PIR motion sensor to detect vehicle movement at the intersection.

Step 3: Install Necessary Libraries

Install Python libraries such as **RPi.GPIO** (for controlling the Raspberry Pi's GPIO pins) and **time** (for timing the traffic light signals).

Step 4: Develop the Algorithm

Write a Python script that controls the traffic lights. The script will use the PIR motion sensor to detect vehicle presence, adjusting the traffic light timings accordingly. If the sensor detects vehicles, the script will keep the green light on longer; if no vehicles are detected, it will shorten the green light duration.

Step 5: Simulate Traffic Flow

Using the PIR motion sensor, simulate traffic flow by triggering the sensor with manual inputs (or simulate it with a timer). Test how the traffic light controller adapts to traffic conditions, adjusting the light timings in real-time.

Step 6: Evaluate and Optimize

Once the system is built and tested, evaluate its performance by monitoring the traffic light timings. Experiment with different configurations, adjusting the timing thresholds and sensor sensitivity to see how the system adapts to various traffic scenarios.

Chapter 7: AI and IoT in Public Safety

In a rapidly evolving urban landscape, ensuring public safety has become a complex, multi-dimensional challenge. The introduction of Artificial Intelligence (AI) and the Internet of Things (IoT) has revolutionized public safety systems, offering unprecedented capabilities for crime detection, emergency response, disaster management, and surveillance. These technologies are no longer just tools for convenience; they are becoming integral components of a robust urban safety infrastructure.

AI, paired with IoT, creates systems capable of real-time data collection, intelligent analysis, and autonomous decision-making, enhancing the efficiency and effectiveness of public safety operations. Whether it's preventing crimes, responding to emergencies, or predicting potential threats, the synergy between AI and IoT allows cities to manage safety proactively rather than reactively.

In this chapter, we will delve deep into how AI and IoT are transforming public safety. From surveillance and crime detection to predictive policing and disaster response, we will explore the applications and technologies that make this transformation possible. Additionally, we will walk through a hands-on project to implement facial recognition for secure access control, showcasing the practical use of AI and IoT in enhancing security.

1. AI and Machine Learning in Surveillance, Crime Detection, and Emergency Response

The integration of AI into surveillance systems has dramatically enhanced their capabilities, transforming them from simple recording devices into smart monitoring tools that can identify, analyze, and respond to security threats autonomously.

AI in Surveillance: From Passive to Active Monitoring

Traditional surveillance systems were limited to passive observation, recording footage that required human intervention for review. AI has introduced a paradigm shift by enabling real-time analysis and decision-making, making surveillance systems much more effective and efficient.

AI-powered surveillance uses machine learning and computer vision to automatically process visual data captured by cameras. These systems can identify faces, detect abnormal behavior, and even recognize objects or movements that are suspicious or out of the ordinary. For example, AI can analyze the flow of crowds, detecting unusual clustering of people or sudden changes in movement patterns—signals of potential trouble.

Key AI-Driven Surveillance Technologies:

1. **Facial Recognition**: One of the most well-known applications of AI in surveillance, facial recognition systems match faces captured by cameras with databases of known individuals. These systems are widely used in security, law enforcement, and even in commercial spaces for identity verification.

2. **Behavioral Analysis**: AI algorithms are capable of analyzing movement patterns within a

camera feed to detect suspicious or aggressive behaviors. For example, AI can recognize when someone is loitering in a restricted area, running, or engaging in a violent altercation. Such behaviors trigger alerts to security personnel, who can respond in real-time.

3. **Object Detection and Tracking**: AI models can be trained to recognize specific objects in video feeds, such as abandoned bags, vehicles left in no-parking zones, or dangerous items like weapons. This provides security teams with actionable insights, significantly improving the speed and accuracy of threat detection.

Example: AI-Powered Surveillance in Smart Cities
Cities like Beijing have implemented AI-driven surveillance systems as part of their public safety infrastructure. Using AI and computer vision, the city monitors public spaces in real time, detecting suspicious behaviors and identifying individuals from surveillance footage using facial recognition. This integration allows law enforcement to respond to security threats in a more timely and targeted manner, potentially preventing crimes before they happen.

AI in Crime Detection and Investigation

AI is not just a tool for surveillance—it's also revolutionizing crime detection and investigation. By analyzing vast amounts of historical data and real-time inputs, AI systems can identify patterns that humans might miss, offering predictive insights into criminal behavior and activity.

- **Predictive Policing**: Machine learning algorithms can be trained on crime data to predict where and when crimes are likely to occur. By analyzing factors such as time of day, location, demographics, and past criminal activity, AI can help law enforcement agencies allocate resources more efficiently, preventing crime in high-risk areas before it happens.

- **Criminal Profiling**: AI can assist in building criminal profiles by analyzing patterns in previous crimes. Using data on behavior, modus operandi, and even psychological patterns, AI can help law enforcement identify potential suspects and link them to a series of unsolved crimes.

- **Automated Report Generation**: AI systems can analyze crime scene reports, witness statements, and forensic data to identify key pieces of information and automatically generate actionable insights. This speeds up the investigative process, reducing the time it takes to solve cases.

AI in Emergency Response

AI has the potential to revolutionize emergency response systems by enabling faster, more accurate decision-making during crises. From natural disasters to medical emergencies, AI and IoT systems allow responders to receive real-time data and make informed decisions about how to allocate resources.

- **Real-Time Incident Detection**: AI systems can process data from emergency calls, video feeds, social media posts, and IoT sensors to detect incidents as they happen. For instance, AI can detect fires by analyzing data from smoke detectors, or track an emergency vehicle's progress using GPS data.

- **Resource Allocation**: AI can optimize emergency response by analyzing real-time data and predicting where resources are needed most. For example, during a fire, AI can help determine which fire stations to deploy based on the fire's location, wind patterns, and available resources.

Example: AI in Emergency Services The city of Los Angeles uses AI to assist its fire department in managing emergency calls. By analyzing past fire data and real-time sensor inputs, AI helps the department dispatch the appropriate resources more effectively. It also predicts which areas are most likely to be affected by a fire based on weather conditions, enabling preventative measures.

2. Integrating AI with IoT for Real-Time Public Safety Monitoring

The integration of IoT with AI in public safety systems enables real-time monitoring and faster response times. IoT devices, such as cameras, sensors, and wearables, collect vast amounts of data, which is processed by AI algorithms to identify threats and provide insights. This data-driven approach allows cities to monitor public safety more effectively, ensuring that law enforcement, medical personnel, and first responders are equipped with the information they need to act quickly.

IoT Devices for Public Safety

1. **Connected Cameras**: Surveillance cameras equipped with AI can automatically analyze video feeds, detect suspicious behavior, and even alert authorities when necessary. These cameras can be placed in high-risk areas, public transport systems, and shopping malls to enhance security.

2. **Environmental Sensors**: IoT sensors can monitor environmental factors such as air quality, radiation levels, and seismic activity, providing valuable information for public safety. These sensors are particularly useful for disaster management, as they can detect hazardous conditions before they become critical.

3. **Wearable Devices for First Responders**: IoT-enabled wearable devices help first responders by monitoring their vital signs and location in real-time. This data is sent to a central command center, ensuring that emergency services are always aware of the health and safety of their personnel.

Real-Time Monitoring with AI and IoT

AI algorithms process data from IoT devices to offer real-time insights into potential threats or emergency situations. In smart cities, this integration enables continuous monitoring of both public spaces and individuals' health, making it easier to respond to incidents as they occur.

Example: Smart Cities with Integrated Safety Systems Cities like New York have implemented IoT-based public safety systems that collect data from thousands of sensors, including traffic cameras, environmental sensors, and wearable devices worn by officers. The collected data is processed in real-time by AI models, providing actionable insights for law enforcement and emergency responders. This integration ensures that the city can respond swiftly to emergencies and reduce response times.

3. Predictive Policing and Disaster Response

AI and IoT are also changing the way we approach long-term public safety by introducing predictive policing and disaster response systems. By analyzing historical data and real-time inputs, these technologies can predict where and when crimes or disasters are likely to occur, enabling law enforcement and emergency services to intervene before events escalate.

Predictive Policing

Predictive policing involves using machine learning algorithms to forecast where crimes are likely to occur based on historical data. By analyzing patterns in crime reports, weather conditions, demographics, and other factors, predictive models can identify hotspots and allocate resources more effectively.

- **Crime Hotspot Detection**: AI can identify patterns in crime data, such as the time of day or location, and predict when and where future crimes are likely to occur. This allows law enforcement to deploy resources more efficiently, preventing crimes before they happen.

- **Targeted Interventions**: Predictive policing can also help identify individuals at high risk of committing crimes, enabling law enforcement to intervene early through social programs or other interventions.

Example: PredPol in Los Angeles PredPol is a predictive policing tool used by the Los Angeles Police Department. By analyzing historical crime data, PredPol predicts where future crimes are likely to occur and helps police officers focus their efforts on high-risk areas. The tool has been credited with reducing crime in several areas of Los Angeles by allowing the department to deploy officers more efficiently.

Disaster Response and Prediction

In addition to crime, AI and IoT are essential in predicting and managing natural disasters. From earthquakes to floods, AI models analyze data from environmental sensors and historical patterns to forecast when disasters are likely to occur.

- **Disaster Prediction**: AI-powered systems can analyze seismic data, weather patterns, and historical disaster records to predict earthquakes, hurricanes, and other natural disasters. This allows emergency services to prepare and evacuate people in high-risk areas ahead of time.

- **Resource Allocation in Emergencies**: AI and IoT devices enable better resource allocation during disasters. For example, drones and robots can be deployed to assess damage in disaster-stricken areas, while AI algorithms predict where help is needed most.

Example: AI and IoT in Earthquake Monitoring Cities in Japan have integrated AI and IoT into their earthquake monitoring systems. IoT sensors detect seismic activity, while AI models analyze the data in real time, providing accurate predictions of the intensity and location of potential earthquakes. These predictions help officials prepare for disasters and evacuate people in high-risk areas before the quake strikes.

4. Hands-On Project: Implementing Facial Recognition for Secure Access Control

Facial recognition technology, powered by AI, is one of the most impactful applications of AI in public safety. It provides a highly secure, automated means of verifying identities in public and private spaces. In this project, we will build a simple facial recognition system that can be used for secure access control. This system can be implemented in various scenarios, such as securing entrances to buildings, controlling access to sensitive areas, or even monitoring public spaces for security purposes.

Step 1: Setting Up the Hardware

To begin this project, you will need:

- **Raspberry Pi** (or similar microcontroller)

- **USB camera** (or Pi Camera Module)

- **Python libraries**: OpenCV, dlib, and face recognition

- **Relay Module** (for controlling access hardware like a door lock)

- **Access Control System** (such as a door or gate)

Step 2: Install Necessary Libraries

Install the required Python libraries for facial recognition:

bash

```
pip install opencv-python
pip install dlib
```

```
pip install face_recognition
```

These libraries will enable you to capture images, detect faces, and match them to a stored database of authorized users.

Step 3: Capture and Train the System

To train the facial recognition system, you need to capture images of the faces that are authorized for access. Set up the camera to take multiple pictures of each person at different angles and store these images in a directory.

Training the Model:

```python
python


import face_recognition

import cv2

import os


# Load known faces

known_faces = []

known_names = []
```

```python
# Capture faces and add to database
for image_path in os.listdir('authorized_faces'):
    image = face_recognition.load_image_file(image_path)
    encoding = face_recognition.face_encodings(image)[0]
    known_faces.append(encoding)
    known_names.append(image_path.split('.')[0])
```

Step 4: Real-Time Face Detection

Using OpenCV, capture video from the camera, detect faces, and compare them to the stored database. If a match is found, trigger the access control system.

Real-Time Face Matching:

python

```python
cap = cv2.VideoCapture(0)


while True:
```

```python
    ret, frame = cap.read()

    rgb_frame = frame[:, :, ::-1]  # Convert frame to RGB

    face_locations =
face_recognition.face_locations(rgb_frame)

    face_encodings =
face_recognition.face_encodings(rgb_frame,
face_locations)


    for (top, right, bottom, left), face_encoding in
zip(face_locations, face_encodings):
        matches =
face_recognition.compare_faces(known_faces,
face_encoding)
        name = "Unknown"


        if True in matches:
            first_match_index = matches.index(True)
            name = known_names[first_match_index]
```

```
    cv2.rectangle(frame, (left, top), (right, bottom), (0,
0, 255), 2)

    cv2.putText(frame, name, (left, top-10),
cv2.FONT_HERSHEY_SIMPLEX, 0.9, (0, 0, 255), 2)


    if name != "Unknown":

        # Trigger access (e.g., unlock door)

        print(f"Access granted for {name}")


    cv2.imshow("Video", frame)


    if cv2.waitKey(1) & 0xFF == ord('q'):

        break


cap.release()

cv2.destroyAllWindows()
```

Step 5: Test the System

Run the system and test it by presenting authorized and unauthorized faces to the camera. The system should only grant access to authorized users, while denying access to unknown faces.

Step 6: Optimize and Extend

Once the system is working, you can optimize it by:

- Adding multiple faces for each user

- Implementing additional authentication methods (e.g., PIN or biometric)

- Integrating the system with a cloud database for remote access control management

Chapter 8: Smart Healthcare: AI in Urban Health Systems

The field of healthcare has undergone a profound transformation with the integration of Artificial Intelligence (AI) and the Internet of Things (IoT). These technologies are fundamentally reshaping how healthcare is delivered, managed, and experienced by patients and providers alike. From AI-powered diagnostics and real-time health monitoring to predictive healthcare and disease prevention, smart healthcare systems are making it possible to offer better care while improving efficiency, accessibility, and patient outcomes. Urban healthcare systems, which face unique challenges due to the density and complexity of cities, are particularly poised to benefit from the convergence of AI and IoT.

In this chapter, we will explore the various ways in which AI and IoT are revolutionizing healthcare in urban environments. We will cover AI applications in hospitals and healthcare facilities, the role of wearable devices and IoT in personalized care, and how AI is used for predictive health and disease prevention. Additionally, we will walk through a hands-on project to build a simple health monitoring IoT device that allows you to collect and analyze health data, giving you practical experience with the technologies that are shaping the future of healthcare.

1. AI in Hospitals, Healthcare Facilities, and Telemedicine

AI is making waves across the entire healthcare sector, from hospitals and healthcare facilities to telemedicine platforms. Its capabilities extend from automating routine tasks to offering decision support in complex medical scenarios, improving patient care, and enhancing operational efficiency.

AI in Hospitals and Healthcare Facilities

AI has become an indispensable tool in modern hospitals, where it helps improve workflow, assist in diagnosis, and streamline administrative processes. AI-powered systems are increasingly used to analyze medical images, predict patient outcomes, and provide personalized treatment recommendations.

AI for Diagnostics and Medical Imaging

AI technologies such as deep learning and computer vision are particularly valuable in diagnostics, where they can be used to analyze medical images (X-rays, MRIs, CT scans) and detect anomalies with a level of precision comparable to, or sometimes exceeding, human specialists. For example, AI algorithms have been trained to detect early signs of diseases like cancer, heart disease, and neurological disorders by analyzing medical imaging data. These AI models can identify patterns that may be difficult for radiologists to spot, improving diagnostic accuracy and reducing the risk of human error.

AI for Clinical Decision Support

AI is also playing a crucial role in clinical decision support systems (CDSS). These systems assist healthcare professionals in making evidence-based decisions by analyzing vast amounts of patient data, including medical records, lab results, and clinical guidelines. AI can recommend personalized treatment plans for patients, taking into account their medical history, risk factors, and even genetic information. This results in more accurate, tailored healthcare, reducing the likelihood of adverse drug interactions or ineffective treatments.

Robotic Process Automation (RPA)

In hospitals and healthcare facilities, AI-driven robotic process automation (RPA) is being deployed to handle administrative tasks such as scheduling, patient registration, and billing. By automating routine tasks, RPA reduces the administrative burden on healthcare workers, allowing them to focus more on patient care.

Example: AI in Radiology in New York's Mount Sinai Health System

Mount Sinai Health System in New York is using AI-powered platforms to assist radiologists in diagnosing medical images. The AI system analyzes images for potential health issues, such as lung cancer or brain tumors, and provides the radiologist with a second opinion. This technology has not only increased diagnostic accuracy but has also helped reduce the time it takes to provide patients with results.

AI in Telemedicine

Telemedicine has witnessed a rapid expansion, especially in the wake of the COVID-19 pandemic, offering patients remote consultations and monitoring. AI plays an essential role in telemedicine by enabling virtual consultations, automating medical transcription, and providing decision support for remote healthcare professionals.

AI-Driven Virtual Health Assistants

AI-powered virtual assistants, such as chatbots or voice assistants, are becoming commonplace in telemedicine. These assistants can triage patient inquiries, offer medical advice based on symptoms, and schedule appointments with healthcare providers. For example, Babylon Health, a UK-based telemedicine platform, uses AI to provide virtual consultations to patients. The AI assistant gathers patient symptoms and offers recommendations for next steps, such as a virtual consultation with a doctor or a referral to a specialist.

Remote Monitoring with AI

In telemedicine, AI is also used for remote patient monitoring. Wearable IoT devices track patients' vital signs, such as heart rate, blood pressure, glucose levels, and oxygen saturation. AI algorithms process this data and alert healthcare providers if a patient's condition deviates from safe thresholds. This allows for continuous monitoring of patients with chronic conditions or those recovering from surgery, providing peace of mind for both the patient and healthcare provider.

Example: AI in Telehealth Services by Teladoc Health

Teladoc Health, a global telemedicine provider, integrates AI into its services to enhance patient care. The company uses AI algorithms to triage patients, determine the urgency of their symptoms, and direct them to the appropriate level of care, whether it be a virtual consultation with a healthcare provider or an in-person visit.

2. Wearable Devices and IoT in Healthcare

Wearable devices and IoT have become integral components of personalized healthcare, enabling patients to monitor their health in real time and providing healthcare providers with valuable data to make informed decisions. These devices have significantly improved the ability to manage chronic diseases, promote wellness, and detect health issues early.

Wearable Devices for Health Monitoring

Wearables are small, portable devices that monitor various physiological parameters, such as heart rate, blood pressure, physical activity, and sleep quality. These devices can connect to smartphones or cloud platforms, allowing users and healthcare providers to track and analyze health data in real time.

- **Smartwatches and Fitness Trackers**: Devices like the Apple Watch, Fitbit, and Garmin are equipped with sensors to track a variety of health metrics. For example, the Apple Watch uses sensors to monitor heart rate, ECG, and blood oxygen levels. In addition, it has a fall detection feature that alerts emergency services if the wearer experiences a serious fall.

- **Continuous Glucose Monitors (CGM)**: For individuals with diabetes, CGMs offer continuous real-time monitoring of blood glucose levels. These wearables use sensors inserted under the skin to measure glucose levels throughout the day, alerting users when their levels are too high or too low.

- **Sleep and Activity Trackers**: IoT-based wearables also track sleep patterns, providing valuable insights into a patient's sleep health. This data can be used to diagnose sleep disorders like sleep apnea, insomnia, and restless leg syndrome.

Remote Patient Monitoring with IoT

Remote patient monitoring (RPM) is a growing field in healthcare, especially for patients with chronic conditions. IoT-enabled medical devices, such as connected blood pressure monitors, thermometers, and stethoscopes, allow healthcare providers to remotely track a patient's condition and intervene when necessary.

Example: Remote Monitoring with Philips HealthSuite

Philips HealthSuite is a connected health platform that enables healthcare providers to remotely monitor patients with chronic conditions. Through wearable IoT devices and sensors, patients' vital signs and other health data are sent in real time to the cloud, where AI algorithms analyze the data and alert healthcare professionals to potential issues.

IoT-Enabled Smart Hospitals

In addition to wearables, IoT is being integrated into healthcare facilities, creating smart hospitals that can track medical equipment, medications, and even hospital beds. Sensors embedded in these assets provide real-time data, ensuring that healthcare professionals have the resources they need when they need them.

- **Smart Beds**: IoT-enabled hospital beds can monitor patients' positions, vital signs, and movement. These beds can alert nursing staff if a patient is at risk of falling or if they require assistance. In addition, smart beds can help hospitals track their inventory, ensuring that each bed is available and ready for use when needed.

- **Smart Medication Dispensers**: These devices ensure that patients receive the right medication at the right time. IoT-enabled dispensers can track medication usage and provide alerts when refills are needed or when doses are missed.

3. AI for Predictive Health and Disease Prevention

One of the most promising areas of AI in healthcare is its ability to predict health issues before they become critical. Predictive health models use AI to analyze large datasets, identify trends, and predict potential health risks, enabling early interventions that can improve patient outcomes and reduce healthcare costs.

Predictive Health Models

AI-powered predictive health models analyze a variety of data sources, including medical records, genetic information, lifestyle factors, and environmental influences, to predict the likelihood of diseases or health events. These models are particularly effective in managing chronic diseases, such as diabetes, cardiovascular disease, and cancer, by identifying individuals who are at high risk and providing them with personalized care plans.

Example: AI for Predicting Heart Disease Risk In cardiovascular care, AI can analyze medical histories, imaging data, and even genetic factors to predict a patient's risk of developing heart disease. By leveraging machine learning algorithms, healthcare providers can identify patients who may benefit from early interventions, such as lifestyle changes, medication, or surgical procedures.

AI for Disease Prevention

AI is also being used in disease prevention by identifying early warning signs of diseases, such as cancer, diabetes, and neurological disorders. By analyzing a combination of medical data and lifestyle factors, AI can recommend preventive measures, such as dietary changes, exercise regimens, or vaccinations.

- **Cancer Detection and Prevention**: AI algorithms can be used to analyze medical images and patient histories to detect early signs of cancer. For example, AI can analyze mammograms to identify abnormalities that might indicate breast cancer, enabling earlier detection and more effective treatment.

- **Predicting and Preventing Diabetes**: AI models can predict a patient's risk of developing type 2 diabetes based on factors such as age, family history, body mass index (BMI), and lifestyle choices. By identifying at-risk individuals early, AI can recommend preventive actions, such as dietary adjustments and increased physical activity.

Example: IBM Watson for Oncology IBM Watson for Oncology uses AI to analyze medical data, including clinical trial data, to provide recommendations for cancer treatment. The system analyzes the patient's medical history and matches it against a large database of case studies and research to provide personalized treatment options.

4. Hands-On Project: Building a Simple Health Monitoring IoT Device

In this hands-on project, we will create a simple health monitoring IoT device that tracks vital signs such as heart rate and body temperature. The device will collect data, send it to a cloud platform for analysis, and provide real-time health updates.

Step 1: Set Up the Hardware

For this project, we will need:

- **Raspberry Pi** or **Arduino** (we will use a Raspberry Pi for this project)

- **Heart rate sensor** (e.g., Pulse Sensor)

- **Temperature sensor** (e.g., DHT11)

- **Wi-Fi module** (for Raspberry Pi, use the built-in Wi-Fi)

- **Cloud platform** (e.g., ThingSpeak or Blynk)

Step 2: Connect the Sensors

Connect the heart rate sensor and temperature sensor to the Raspberry Pi or Arduino according to the pinout diagram. Ensure that the sensors are properly calibrated and working correctly before proceeding.

Step 3: Set Up the Cloud Platform

Create an account on a cloud platform like ThingSpeak or Blynk. These platforms allow you to store, visualize, and analyze health data remotely.

Step 4: Write the Code

Write a Python script (for Raspberry Pi) that reads data from the heart rate and temperature sensors. Use the requests library to send the data to the cloud platform in real-time.

python

```
import time
```

```python
import requests

import Adafruit_DHT


# Set up sensors

DHT_SENSOR = Adafruit_DHT.DHT11

DHT_PIN = 4  # GPIO pin for the temperature sensor


# Cloud API endpoint

url = "https://api.thingspeak.com/update?api_key=YOUR_API_KEY"


while True:
    # Read temperature and humidity

    humidity, temperature = Adafruit_DHT.read(DHT_SENSOR, DHT_PIN)

    if humidity is not None and temperature is not None:

        # Send data to ThingSpeak
```

```
    payload = {"field1": temperature, "field2":
humidity}

    response = requests.get(url, params=payload)

    print(f"Sent data: Temp={temperature}C,
Humidity={humidity}%")

  else:

    print("Failed to retrieve data from sensor")



  time.sleep(60)  # Wait for a minute before sending
next data
```

Step 5: Test the Device

Once the device is set up, test it by running the code and verifying that the data is being sent to the cloud platform. You should be able to see real-time updates of the heart rate and temperature data on your cloud dashboard.

Step 6: Visualize the Data

Use the cloud platform's dashboard to visualize the collected health data in real-time. You can display graphs, set up alerts for abnormal readings, and analyze trends in patient health data.

Chapter 9: Sustainability and Green Smart Cities

As the global population continues to grow, and as urbanization accelerates, cities face an increasing pressure to develop sustainably. The rapid expansion of urban areas places an enormous strain on natural resources, environmental systems, and the infrastructure designed to support urban life. In response, the concept of "smart cities" has evolved to not only focus on technology and efficiency but also on sustainability, transforming urban spaces into more energy-efficient, resource-conserving, and environmentally-friendly environments.

In the context of smart cities, Artificial Intelligence (AI) and the Internet of Things (IoT) are the cornerstones of sustainable urban development. These technologies enable cities to collect, analyze, and act on vast amounts of data in real time, creating more efficient systems for waste management, water conservation, energy use, and even urban agriculture. In this chapter, we will explore how AI and IoT are driving the creation of green, sustainable cities and how these technologies are transforming various urban sectors, from waste management to smart buildings, green energy, and urban agriculture. Additionally, we will walk through a hands-on project to design a smart irrigation system using IoT, which serves as a model for efficient resource use and sustainability.

1. AI and IoT in Waste Management, Water Conservation, and Energy Efficiency

One of the most critical areas where AI and IoT are making a profound impact is in the efficient use of resources, such as waste, water, and energy. These sectors have traditionally been plagued by inefficiencies, waste, and a lack of real-time data, but the integration of AI and IoT is changing the way cities manage these vital resources.

AI and IoT in Waste Management

In traditional waste management systems, garbage collection is typically scheduled, and trucks follow predefined routes, whether or not the containers are full. This leads to inefficiencies, increased costs, and unnecessary pollution. With the advent of IoT and AI, waste management is becoming more efficient, smart, and environmentally friendly.

- **Smart Bins**: IoT-enabled smart waste bins are equipped with sensors that monitor the fill levels of trash containers in real-time. These sensors send data to waste management systems, which can then optimize collection schedules. By only sending trucks to pick up bins that are full, cities can reduce fuel consumption, emissions, and labor costs. These systems also allow for a more streamlined waste management process, improving the overall sustainability of urban areas.

- **Waste Sorting and Recycling**: AI-driven waste sorting systems use computer vision and machine learning to identify recyclable materials in mixed waste. These systems can automatically separate plastic, metal, paper, and other materials, improving recycling rates and reducing contamination. In addition, machine learning algorithms can predict the types of waste that will be generated in different areas, helping cities adjust their waste management strategies accordingly.

Example: Smart Waste Management in Seoul

Seoul, South Korea, has implemented a smart waste management system that uses IoT sensors in waste bins to monitor their fill levels and sends real-time data to a central platform. The city has also integrated AI-powered systems to optimize collection routes, ensuring that waste is collected only when needed, reducing the number of waste trucks on the roads and minimizing carbon emissions.

Water Conservation with IoT and AI

Water is one of the most precious resources in any city, and managing it efficiently is crucial for sustainability. AI and IoT are playing a transformative role in helping cities conserve water and ensure its equitable distribution.

- **Smart Water Meters**: IoT-enabled smart water meters provide real-time monitoring of water usage in homes, businesses, and industries. These meters can detect leaks, track consumption patterns, and provide users with detailed information on their water usage. By collecting data on water consumption, utilities can optimize distribution, reduce waste, and provide consumers with actionable insights into how they can save water.

- **Leak Detection and Prevention**: IoT sensors installed in water pipes can detect leaks and send alerts to utilities, allowing for prompt repairs. AI algorithms analyze data from these sensors to predict when and where leaks are likely to occur, reducing water loss and ensuring that water distribution systems are running optimally.

- **Smart Irrigation**: Smart irrigation systems use IoT sensors to monitor soil moisture levels, weather forecasts, and environmental conditions. These systems automatically adjust watering schedules to ensure that plants are receiving the right amount of water at the right time, reducing water waste and promoting efficient water usage in agricultural and landscaping settings.

Example: Water Conservation in Barcelona

Barcelona has integrated smart water meters and leak detection systems across the city to reduce water consumption. IoT sensors continuously monitor the city's water distribution network, and AI algorithms analyze the data to predict potential leaks and optimize water flow. The city has achieved significant reductions in water waste through this system, making it a model for urban water conservation.

Energy Efficiency in Smart Cities

Cities are major consumers of energy, and improving energy efficiency is one of the most important factors in building sustainable urban environments. AI and IoT enable cities to manage energy usage more effectively, reduce waste, and promote the use of renewable energy sources.

- **Smart Grids**: Smart grids use IoT devices to monitor and control energy distribution across the city. These systems collect real-time data on energy consumption and adjust the flow of electricity to where it is needed most. AI is used to forecast energy demand, optimize energy distribution, and even integrate renewable energy sources, such as solar and wind, into the grid. By doing so, smart grids help reduce energy waste, lower costs, and enhance the overall efficiency of the urban energy system.

- **Smart Buildings**: IoT-enabled smart buildings are designed to minimize energy consumption by optimizing heating, cooling, and lighting based on occupancy and environmental conditions. AI algorithms predict energy usage patterns and adjust systems to ensure that energy is used efficiently. Smart buildings also collect data on energy consumption, enabling building managers to identify areas where improvements can be made.

- **Demand Response**: AI systems can predict peak energy demand and adjust the distribution of energy accordingly. By managing demand in real time, cities can reduce the need for additional power plants, lower energy costs, and decrease carbon emissions.

Example: Smart Grid in New York City New York City's Con Edison utility company has implemented a smart grid system that uses IoT devices to monitor energy consumption and optimize the flow of electricity. The system integrates renewable energy sources and provides real-time data on energy demand, enabling the utility to balance supply and demand efficiently.

2. Sustainable Urban Agriculture and Smart Ecosystems

As cities grow, urban agriculture has become an increasingly important solution for ensuring food security, reducing food miles, and promoting sustainability. AI and IoT technologies are enabling the development of smart ecosystems for urban farming, allowing for more efficient food production, resource management, and waste reduction.

Urban Agriculture and Vertical Farming

Urban agriculture involves growing food in cities, either in community gardens or on rooftops. Vertical farming, a method of growing crops in stacked layers, is particularly suited for urban environments where space is limited. AI and IoT are playing key roles in optimizing these farming methods, increasing yields while reducing resource consumption.

- **IoT-Enabled Vertical Farms**: In vertical farms, IoT sensors monitor various environmental conditions, such as temperature, humidity, light levels, and CO_2 concentrations. These sensors help optimize the growing conditions for plants, ensuring that they receive the perfect amount of water, nutrients, and light. AI algorithms analyze the data and make real-time adjustments to optimize plant growth and reduce resource usage.

- **Automated Farming Systems**: AI-driven robotics are being used to automate farming tasks such as planting, watering, and harvesting. These systems reduce the need for human labor, increase efficiency, and allow for large-scale production in urban settings.

Example: Vertical Farming in Singapore Singapore has become a leader in vertical farming, with companies like Sky Greens utilizing IoT sensors and AI algorithms to optimize crop production in high-rise buildings. These smart farms use minimal water and energy, reducing the environmental impact of food production while maximizing yields in the limited urban space available.

Smart Ecosystems and Circular Economy

A smart ecosystem in the context of a city refers to a system where various components of the urban environment work together to optimize resource use and minimize waste. This is often referred to as a circular economy, where materials and resources are continuously reused, and waste is minimized.

- **Waste-to-Energy Systems**: IoT and AI are used to optimize waste-to-energy systems, where organic waste is converted into energy through processes like anaerobic digestion. These systems help reduce the amount of waste that ends up in landfills while providing a renewable energy source for the city.

- **Urban Green Spaces**: IoT sensors are used to monitor urban green spaces, ensuring that they are well-maintained and contribute to the city's environmental health. These sensors track factors like soil moisture, air quality, and plant health, providing data that can be used to improve the management of parks and green spaces.

Example: Smart Ecosystem in Copenhagen

Copenhagen has implemented a range of smart city

technologies to create a circular economy. The city uses IoT to monitor and optimize energy usage, waste management, and water consumption, with a particular focus on reducing environmental impact. The integration of AI-powered systems has allowed Copenhagen to significantly reduce its carbon footprint, making it one of the most sustainable cities in the world.

3. Smart Buildings and Green Energy Solutions

Smart buildings are a cornerstone of sustainable urban development. By integrating IoT and AI, smart buildings can minimize energy consumption, reduce operational costs, and improve the comfort and safety of occupants. These buildings are designed to be energy-efficient, resilient, and environmentally friendly, contributing to the overall sustainability of urban areas.

Energy-Efficient Building Systems

AI and IoT technologies are used in smart buildings to optimize heating, ventilation, and air conditioning (HVAC) systems, lighting, and energy use. These systems adjust based on occupancy and external conditions, ensuring that energy is used only when needed and reducing waste.

- **Smart HVAC Systems**: AI-powered HVAC systems use IoT sensors to monitor the temperature, humidity, and air quality in different parts of the building. The system adjusts heating and cooling settings automatically to ensure comfort while minimizing energy consumption.

- **Smart Lighting**: Smart lighting systems use motion sensors and AI algorithms to adjust lighting levels based on occupancy and natural light availability. These systems can also be programmed to automatically turn off lights when rooms are unoccupied, reducing energy waste.

Green Energy Solutions

Smart buildings are also increasingly being integrated with renewable energy solutions, such as solar panels, wind turbines, and energy storage systems. AI and IoT are used to monitor energy production, storage, and consumption, ensuring that renewable energy is utilized efficiently and that buildings remain energy-independent.

- **Building-Integrated Photovoltaics (BIPV)**: BIPV systems integrate solar panels directly into the building's structure, such as on rooftops or facades. IoT sensors monitor energy production, while AI algorithms optimize energy storage and usage, reducing reliance on the grid.

- **Energy Storage Systems**: Smart buildings use energy storage systems to store excess energy produced by renewable sources for use during peak demand periods. AI optimizes the charging and discharging cycles of these storage systems to ensure that energy is available when needed most.

Example: The Edge in Amsterdam The Edge, a smart building in Amsterdam, is one of the most sustainable office buildings in the world. It uses a combination of IoT sensors, AI algorithms, and renewable energy sources to optimize energy use and reduce waste. The building is designed to maximize energy efficiency, with solar panels, smart HVAC systems, and a green roof that provides insulation and reduces heat absorption.

4. Hands-On Project: Designing a Smart Irrigation System Using IoT

In this project, we will design a simple smart irrigation system using IoT technology. This system will automatically water plants based on real-time soil moisture readings, optimizing water usage and contributing to sustainability. By integrating sensors, IoT devices, and cloud platforms, we can create an efficient irrigation system that conserves water and reduces waste.

Step 1: Set Up the Hardware

You will need the following components:

- **Microcontroller** (e.g., Arduino or Raspberry Pi)

- **Soil moisture sensor** (e.g., capacitive or resistive sensor)

- **Water pump** or **solenoid valve** for irrigation control

- **Relay module** to control the water pump

- **Wi-Fi module** (e.g., ESP8266) for cloud connectivity

- **Cloud platform** (e.g., ThingSpeak or Blynk) to store and visualize data

Step 2: Connect the Sensors

Connect the soil moisture sensor to the microcontroller to measure the moisture level of the soil. Also, connect the water pump or solenoid valve to the relay module, which will allow you to control the water flow programmatically.

Step 3: Write the Code

Write a script to monitor the soil moisture levels using the sensor. When the moisture level falls below a specified threshold, the system will automatically activate the water pump to irrigate the plants.

cpp

```cpp
#include <ESP8266WiFi.h>

#include <ThingSpeak.h>


const int soilMoisturePin = A0;

const int relayPin = D1;

WiFiClient client;
```

```
void setup() {

  pinMode(soilMoisturePin, INPUT);

  pinMode(relayPin, OUTPUT);

  WiFi.begin("yourSSID", "yourPassword");

  ThingSpeak.begin(client);

}


void loop() {

  int soilMoistureValue = analogRead(soilMoisturePin);

  if (soilMoistureValue < 500) {

    digitalWrite(relayPin, HIGH); // Turn on water pump

  } else {

    digitalWrite(relayPin, LOW); // Turn off water pump

  }


  ThingSpeak.setField(1, soilMoistureValue);
```

```
ThingSpeak.writeFields(yourChannelID,
"yourWriteAPIKey");

  delay(60000); // Wait 1 minute before checking again

}
```

Step 4: Set Up the Cloud Platform

Set up a cloud platform like ThingSpeak to monitor and analyze the data in real time. Create a dashboard to visualize soil moisture levels and track irrigation events.

Step 5: Test the System

Once the system is set up, test it by adjusting the soil moisture and observing how the system automatically activates the irrigation pump when moisture levels are low. Verify that the data is being sent to the cloud and displayed in real-time.

Chapter 10: The Future of Mobility: Autonomous Vehicles and AI

The future of urban mobility is rapidly evolving with the advent of autonomous vehicles (AVs), self-driving cars, drones, and AI-powered public transportation systems. These transformative technologies are poised to revolutionize how we move within cities, enhancing efficiency, safety, and accessibility. As AI continues to drive innovation in the transportation sector, cities worldwide are facing the challenge of integrating autonomous systems into their existing infrastructure while addressing key concerns like safety, regulation, and societal impact.

In this chapter, we will explore the role of AI in shaping the future of mobility, particularly in urban environments. We will look at autonomous vehicles and drones, AI's role in self-driving cars and public transport systems, and the challenges and solutions for integrating these technologies into cities. Furthermore, we will walk through a hands-on project where you will design a basic autonomous robot capable of navigation, providing you with practical experience in building autonomous systems.

1. Autonomous Vehicles in Urban Settings

Autonomous vehicles (AVs) represent one of the most significant advancements in transportation technology. These vehicles use a combination of sensors, machine learning algorithms, and advanced control systems to navigate without human intervention. In urban settings, AVs promise to alleviate congestion, reduce accidents, and create a more efficient and sustainable transportation system.

How Autonomous Vehicles Work

Autonomous vehicles rely on a suite of technologies to perceive their environment, make decisions, and safely navigate urban landscapes. These technologies include:

- **Sensors**: AVs are equipped with an array of sensors, including LiDAR (Light Detection and Ranging), radar, cameras, and ultrasonic sensors, to create a detailed map of the vehicle's surroundings. LiDAR, for example, provides high-resolution 3D images of the environment, helping the vehicle detect obstacles, pedestrians, and other vehicles.

- **Computer Vision and AI**: The cameras on AVs capture images that are processed using computer vision algorithms to identify and classify objects, such as traffic signals, pedestrians, and road signs. AI and machine learning play a crucial role in helping the vehicle understand its environment and make real-time decisions based on the data collected from sensors.

- **Simultaneous Localization and Mapping (SLAM)**: SLAM is a technique used by autonomous vehicles to build and update maps of their surroundings while simultaneously tracking their location. This technology is particularly useful for navigating in complex urban environments where GPS signals might be weak or unavailable.

- **Control Systems and Decision Making**: AVs use complex algorithms to control the vehicle's movements, including steering, braking, and acceleration. These systems take into account inputs from sensors and AI models to make decisions on how to navigate the road safely.

Urban Mobility Challenges and Opportunities for AVs

Urban environments present unique challenges for autonomous vehicles. Unlike highways, cities are full of dynamic and unpredictable elements, such as pedestrians, cyclists, public transport vehicles, and construction zones. Autonomous vehicles must navigate these elements while ensuring passenger safety and adhering to traffic rules.

- **Challenges**:
  - **Complex Road Environments**: Urban roads often feature a variety of unpredictable situations, such as jaywalking pedestrians, cyclists weaving

through traffic, or construction zones that block lanes. AVs must be able to navigate these environments with precision and safety.

- **Traffic Signals and Infrastructure**: While traffic lights and signs are standard in most cities, not all roads are equipped with modern, consistent signage. Autonomous vehicles must be able to interpret and react to different types of traffic signals and road markings.

- **Weather Conditions**: Inclement weather, such as fog, rain, or snow, can hinder sensor performance, making it more difficult for AVs to detect obstacles and navigate safely. AI systems must be designed to adapt to changing weather conditions to maintain reliable performance.

- **Opportunities**:

  - **Reduced Traffic Congestion**: Autonomous vehicles can communicate with each other and traffic management systems to optimize traffic flow, reducing congestion. By coordinating vehicle movements, AVs can ensure smoother traffic patterns and minimize delays.

- ○ **Improved Safety**: AI-powered AVs are designed to eliminate human error, which is responsible for a significant percentage of traffic accidents. By using sensors and real-time decision-making, AVs can respond faster than human drivers and reduce the likelihood of accidents caused by distraction, fatigue, or impaired driving.

- ○ **Environmental Benefits**: Autonomous vehicles can optimize driving patterns, such as acceleration and braking, leading to fuel savings and reduced emissions. Additionally, AVs can be integrated into electric vehicle (EV) fleets, further reducing their environmental impact.

Example: Waymo's Autonomous Taxi Service in Phoenix Waymo, the autonomous vehicle subsidiary of Alphabet (Google's parent company), has launched a fully autonomous taxi service in Phoenix, Arizona. Using a fleet of self-driving cars, Waymo offers passengers a driverless experience, leveraging AI and sensors to navigate the city's streets. The service has been running for several years and provides insights into the practical application of AVs in urban environments.

2. AI's Role in Self-Driving Cars, Drones, and Public Transport

AI plays a pivotal role in enabling the functionality of autonomous systems across various modes of transportation, including self-driving cars, drones, and public transport.

AI in Self-Driving Cars

As mentioned earlier, self-driving cars use a combination of AI, machine learning, and sensors to navigate their environment and make decisions. AI is used to process data from the vehicle's sensors, interpret the surrounding environment, and make decisions in real time. For example, AI can determine the best course of action when encountering a pedestrian crossing the street, adjusting speed and trajectory to ensure safety.

- **Behavior Prediction**: AI is used to predict the behavior of other road users, such as pedestrians, cyclists, and other drivers. By analyzing past behavior patterns, AI can anticipate potential risks and take preventative actions, such as slowing down or changing lanes.

- **Path Planning**: AI systems continuously optimize the vehicle's route, considering traffic conditions, road closures, and the vehicle's destination. AI algorithms help the vehicle make split-second decisions on navigation, ensuring it takes the safest and most efficient route.

AI in Drones for Delivery and Surveillance

Drones, or unmanned aerial vehicles (UAVs), are another rapidly advancing technology that benefits from AI. Drones are used for a variety of tasks in urban settings, including delivery services, surveillance, and infrastructure inspection.

- **Autonomous Navigation**: AI enables drones to fly autonomously, making decisions in real-time about route adjustments, avoiding obstacles, and landing safely. Computer vision and AI algorithms allow drones to detect and avoid objects in their path, ensuring safe navigation in dynamic environments.

- **Delivery Drones**: Companies like Amazon and UPS are testing drone delivery systems that use AI to autonomously transport packages to customers in urban areas. AI helps drones optimize their flight paths, avoid no-fly zones, and ensure that deliveries are completed in a timely manner.

- **Surveillance and Monitoring**: Drones are also used for urban surveillance, monitoring traffic, construction sites, or public events. AI systems process the data collected by drone cameras to detect unusual activities or potential security threats.

Example: Amazon Prime Air Amazon's Prime Air drone delivery service uses AI to autonomously navigate the skies, delivering packages to customers in urban environments. The drones use machine learning algorithms to avoid obstacles, adjust flight paths in real time, and deliver packages to specific locations.

AI in Public Transport

Autonomous systems are not limited to private vehicles and drones—public transport systems are also integrating AI to enhance efficiency and passenger experience.

- **Autonomous Buses**: Several cities are experimenting with autonomous buses that can navigate through traffic, pick up and drop off passengers, and adapt to changing routes. AI algorithms enable these buses to interact with passengers, adapt to schedule changes, and avoid obstacles in crowded urban environments.

- **Smart Traffic Management for Public Transport**: AI can optimize public transport systems by predicting demand, adjusting schedules, and managing capacity. For example, AI can analyze real-time passenger data to predict when buses or trains will be crowded and adjust schedules accordingly to avoid overcrowding.

- **AI in Route Optimization**: Public transport systems use AI to optimize routes based on real-time traffic data and passenger demand. By continuously analyzing traffic patterns and passenger volume, AI can suggest alternative routes and schedules, improving the overall efficiency of the system.

Example: Autonomous Buses in Helsinki Helsinki, Finland, has deployed autonomous buses as part of its smart city initiative. These buses use AI to navigate through city streets, picking up passengers and adjusting routes as needed. The system has shown promising results, enhancing the city's public transport system and reducing carbon emissions.

3. Challenges and Solutions for Integrating Autonomous Systems into Cities

While the potential benefits of autonomous systems in urban mobility are immense, the integration of these technologies into existing city infrastructure comes with several challenges. These challenges range from technical issues to regulatory concerns, public acceptance, and ethical considerations.

Challenges in Integrating Autonomous Systems

1. **Infrastructure Readiness**: Many urban environments were not designed to accommodate autonomous vehicles. For AVs to operate effectively, cities must invest in

infrastructure upgrades, such as smart traffic lights, dedicated lanes for AVs, and improved road markings. Ensuring that AVs can interact seamlessly with existing infrastructure is one of the key hurdles to widespread adoption.

2. **Public Safety and Trust**: While autonomous systems are designed to be safer than human drivers, there is still public skepticism about their reliability and safety. High-profile accidents involving autonomous vehicles have raised concerns about the readiness of AVs for real-world deployment. Building trust in these systems is critical to their acceptance.

3. **Regulatory and Legal Frameworks**: Governments around the world are still working to develop regulatory frameworks for autonomous vehicles. These frameworks must address a wide range of issues, including liability in case of accidents, insurance requirements, and safety standards. Additionally, cities must consider how to integrate autonomous systems with existing public transportation networks and services.

4. **Ethical Considerations**: Autonomous systems raise a number of ethical questions, particularly when it comes to decision-making in emergency situations. For example, if an AV must choose between hitting a pedestrian or swerving into a wall, how should it make that decision? AI systems need to be designed with ethical guidelines that align with societal values.

Solutions for Overcoming Challenges

1. **Infrastructure Upgrades**: Cities can work with AV manufacturers to update traffic systems, road signs, and infrastructure to support autonomous vehicles. This may include installing smart traffic lights that communicate with AVs, creating dedicated lanes for AVs, and updating road markings to make them more visible to sensors.

2. **Public Education and Trust-Building**: Public outreach and education are essential to building trust in autonomous vehicles. Cities can implement pilot programs to demonstrate the safety and efficiency of AVs, allowing citizens to experience the technology firsthand.

3. **Collaborative Regulation**: Governments, AV manufacturers, and transportation experts must work together to create comprehensive and adaptable regulatory frameworks for autonomous vehicles. These regulations should ensure the safe deployment of AVs while addressing concerns related to insurance, liability, and data privacy.

4. **Ethical AI Systems**: Developers of autonomous systems must integrate ethical decision-making frameworks into AI algorithms. These systems should be designed to prioritize human life, safety, and fairness in all decision-making processes.

4. Hands-On Project: Building a Basic Autonomous Robot for Navigation

In this project, we will build a basic autonomous robot that can navigate through an environment, avoid obstacles, and reach a designated destination. This robot will serve as a simplified version of an autonomous vehicle and provide insight into how these systems work in practice.

Step 1: Set Up the Hardware

For this project, you will need:

- **Microcontroller** (e.g., Arduino or Raspberry Pi)
- **DC motors** with motor driver shield
- **Ultrasonic sensors** for obstacle detection
- **Chassis** (robot frame)
- **Wheels and tires**
- **Power supply** (e.g., battery pack)

Step 2: Assemble the Robot

Connect the motors to the motor driver shield and attach them to the chassis. Mount the ultrasonic sensors to the front of the robot to detect obstacles in its path. Connect the sensors and motors to the microcontroller.

Step 3: Write the Code

Write a program that enables the robot to move forward until it detects an obstacle. When an obstacle is detected, the robot should stop, turn, and continue moving until it reaches its destination.

cpp

```
#include <NewPing.h>


#define TRIG_PIN 12

#define ECHO_PIN 11

#define MAX_DISTANCE 200

NewPing sonar(TRIG_PIN, ECHO_PIN,
MAX_DISTANCE);


void setup() {
  pinMode(9, OUTPUT); // Right motor
  pinMode(10, OUTPUT); // Left motor
  Serial.begin(9600);
}


void loop() {
  int distance = sonar.ping_cm();
  if (distance > 10 && distance < 100) {
```

```
    forward();

  } else {

    turn();

  }

}


void forward() {

  digitalWrite(9, HIGH);

  digitalWrite(10, HIGH);

}


void turn() {

  digitalWrite(9, LOW);

  digitalWrite(10, HIGH); // Turn left

}
```

Step 4: Test the Robot

Upload the code to the microcontroller and test the robot. Place it in an environment with obstacles and observe how it navigates autonomously, avoiding obstacles and continuing its path.

Step 5: Optimization

You can optimize the robot by adding more sensors, improving its navigation algorithm, and enabling it to follow a specific path or destination. Experiment with different sensor placements and movement strategies to improve the robot's performance.

This hands-on project demonstrates the fundamental concepts behind autonomous navigation, and by extending it, you can build a more sophisticated autonomous robot. The principles you learn here are directly applicable to autonomous vehicles and other self-driving systems, helping you understand the challenges and opportunities in this exciting field. Through this project and the broader concepts covered in the chapter, you are now equipped with the knowledge to navigate the future of mobility powered by AI and autonomous systems.

Chapter 11: Human-Robot Interaction in Smart Cities

As cities evolve into smarter, more interconnected environments, one of the most promising developments is the integration of robots into urban life. These robots, powered by Artificial Intelligence (AI), are designed to assist with a wide array of tasks, from public safety to healthcare, and even environmental monitoring. Human-Robot Interaction (HRI) plays a crucial role in determining how these robots will function alongside humans, especially as we move towards increasingly autonomous and collaborative robots in our daily lives.

In this chapter, we will explore the fundamentals of Human-Robot Interaction in the context of smart cities. We will discuss how robots can be designed to interact seamlessly with humans in urban environments, the role of AI in facilitating communication and collaboration between robots and humans, and the ethical considerations surrounding these interactions. Finally, we will walk through a hands-on project, where you will program a robot to assist with simple tasks, gaining practical experience in creating robots that can interact effectively with people.

1. Designing Robots for Interaction with Humans in Urban Environments

The integration of robots into urban settings requires careful consideration of how they will interact with people in diverse and dynamic environments. Robots must be designed not only to perform tasks efficiently but also to engage with humans in a way that is intuitive, safe, and acceptable to the public.

Robots for Public Service and Assistance

Robots are increasingly being deployed in urban settings to assist with tasks ranging from delivering goods to providing assistance in public spaces. These robots must be designed to navigate crowded environments, avoid obstacles, and communicate effectively with humans.

Examples of Public Service Robots:

- **Delivery Robots**: Autonomous delivery robots are being used to transport goods across cities. These robots must interact with pedestrians and other vehicles, responding to changes in the environment and avoiding collisions. For example, robots used for food delivery navigate sidewalks and crosswalks, using sensors and AI algorithms to detect pedestrians, cyclists, and other obstacles.

- **Service Robots in Healthcare**: In hospitals, robots assist with tasks such as delivering medication, cleaning, and guiding patients to their destinations. These robots must navigate busy hospital corridors and interact with patients, healthcare workers, and visitors in a non-intrusive manner.

- **Security Robots**: Robots used for public safety must be able to patrol urban spaces, interact with the public, and respond to potential threats. These robots need to be designed to engage with people, explain their tasks, and respond appropriately to emergency situations.

Designing for Social Interaction

Urban robots are expected to interact socially with humans, whether in service roles or as companions. To achieve effective HRI, robots must understand human behavior, communicate in a manner that feels natural, and respond to emotional cues.

Key Aspects of Socially Interactive Robots:

- **Speech and Language Processing**: Robots designed to interact with humans in smart cities often incorporate natural language processing (NLP) capabilities, allowing them to understand and respond to voice commands. These robots can use conversational AI to offer assistance, explain their functions, or provide information in a manner that mimics human interaction.

- **Non-Verbal Communication**: Robots also use non-verbal communication, such as facial expressions, body language, and visual cues, to convey messages. For example, a robot designed for public service might wave when it completes a task or display an animated face to indicate emotions like friendliness or frustration.

- **Behavioral Adaptation**: Robots must adapt their behavior to the context and the individuals they interact with. For example, a robot in a busy urban setting may need to adjust its speed or path based on the density of foot traffic, ensuring that it doesn't interfere with pedestrians.

Navigating Dynamic Urban Environments

Unlike controlled environments such as factories or warehouses, urban environments are complex and dynamic. Robots designed for urban settings must navigate unpredictable scenarios, including crowds, vehicles, and changes in the environment such as construction zones, road closures, or unexpected obstacles.

Key Design Considerations for Navigation:

- **Autonomous Navigation**: Robots use a variety of sensors, including LiDAR, cameras, and ultrasonic sensors, to map their environment in real time and navigate around obstacles. Autonomous robots must be able to process vast amounts of data and make decisions on the fly to avoid collisions and navigate safely.

- **Localization and Path Planning**: Using AI-powered systems, robots must continuously determine their position within the environment and calculate the optimal path to their destination. In crowded spaces, robots must be able to adapt their paths dynamically, taking into account pedestrian movement, obstacles, and changes in traffic patterns.

2. AI's Role in Communication and Collaboration Between Humans and Robots

Artificial Intelligence plays a pivotal role in enabling robots to communicate effectively with humans and collaborate seamlessly in urban environments. From understanding natural language to interpreting social cues and making real-time decisions, AI is the brain that powers robot interactions.

Natural Language Processing (NLP) and Speech Recognition

A critical component of HRI is the ability for robots to understand and generate human language. Natural Language Processing (NLP) allows robots to interpret spoken or written language, enabling communication between robots and humans in a natural, intuitive way.

- **Speech Recognition**: Robots use speech recognition algorithms to convert spoken language into text, allowing them to understand voice commands or conversational exchanges. For example, robots used in smart cities can respond to requests for directions, order fulfillment, or service updates through voice commands.

- **Text-to-Speech (TTS)**: Once the robot has understood a command, it must communicate back in a human-understandable format. Text-to-speech systems allow robots to "speak" back to users in a clear, natural voice.

Example: AI Chatbots for Customer Service AI chatbots and voice assistants, like Amazon's Alexa or Apple's Siri, serve as examples of how AI can facilitate communication between humans and machines. These systems are being adapted for robots in urban environments, enabling them to engage in conversations with users, answer questions, and provide helpful information.

Computer Vision and Emotional Intelligence

In addition to language, robots need to understand human behavior and emotions. AI algorithms that process visual data, such as facial expressions and body language, allow robots to interact with humans in socially appropriate ways.

- **Facial Recognition**: Robots equipped with facial recognition software can identify and remember individuals, creating personalized experiences. For example, robots in public spaces can recognize returning users and greet them by name, enhancing customer service interactions.

- **Emotion Recognition**: Advanced AI models are capable of detecting emotions from facial expressions, tone of voice, and body language. By interpreting emotional cues, robots can respond in ways that are empathetic and supportive, making interactions more pleasant and effective.

Collaborative AI in Team Environments

In many urban settings, robots do not work in isolation but rather as part of a team, either collaborating with humans or other robots. AI enables these collaborative interactions, allowing robots to function as part of a larger ecosystem.

- **Task Delegation**: Collaborative robots (cobots) are designed to work alongside humans, often assisting with heavy lifting, repetitive tasks, or precise operations. AI systems help robots coordinate with human teammates, ensuring that tasks are performed efficiently and safely.

- **Multi-Robot Coordination**: In some environments, such as warehouses, hospitals, or public spaces, multiple robots may work together. AI systems coordinate their actions, ensuring that robots avoid interference with each other, share information, and complete tasks cooperatively.

Example: Boston Dynamics' Spot Robots Boston Dynamics' Spot robots are a prime example of collaborative robots. In various settings, from construction sites to hospitals, Spot robots use AI to coordinate with other robots and humans. These robots can carry heavy loads, navigate complex environments, and work alongside human operators in collaborative environments.

3. Human-Robot Trust and Ethical Considerations

While AI and robots offer immense potential, they also introduce complex ethical issues that must be addressed as these technologies become more integrated into urban life. A crucial factor in ensuring successful Human-Robot Interaction is building trust between humans and robots. For robots to be accepted and relied upon, they must be transparent, reliable, and behave ethically.

Building Trust in Autonomous Systems

For robots to operate effectively in human environments, they must earn and maintain trust. Trust is particularly important in scenarios where robots perform critical tasks, such as healthcare, security, or transportation. Humans must trust that robots will act safely, follow rules, and make decisions that align with societal norms.

- **Transparency**: One of the key factors in building trust is transparency. Humans need to understand how robots make decisions and how their systems work. AI models must be explainable, meaning that humans can understand why a robot made a certain decision or took a particular action.

- **Reliability**: Trust is built through consistent, reliable performance. Robots in urban environments must demonstrate a high level of reliability, ensuring that they can perform tasks without failure, especially in critical applications like healthcare, public safety, and transportation.

Ethical Challenges in HRI

Ethical considerations play a crucial role in Human-Robot Interaction, especially as robots take on more autonomous roles in society.

- **Privacy**: Robots equipped with sensors and cameras can collect sensitive data, including personal information, behavioral patterns, and even emotions. Safeguarding this data and ensuring that robots respect user privacy is essential to fostering trust.

- **Bias and Fairness**: AI algorithms must be designed to avoid biases that could lead to unfair treatment of individuals or groups. In public-facing applications like healthcare, transportation, and law enforcement, robots must ensure that their decision-making processes are fair and equitable.

- **Accountability**: As robots become more autonomous, questions of accountability arise. If a robot makes a mistake, who is responsible? Clear guidelines and legal frameworks must be established to address these issues.

Regulating AI and Robotics in Urban Environments

Governments and regulatory bodies must establish rules and regulations to ensure that robots are deployed ethically and safely in urban environments. These regulations should address issues such as:

- **Safety Standards**: Robots must adhere to safety standards that protect human life and property. These standards ensure that robots can operate safely in public spaces and interact with people without causing harm.

- **Ethical Guidelines for Decision-Making**: Robots should be programmed with ethical decision-making frameworks that align with societal values. For example, robots used in healthcare should prioritize patient welfare and adhere to medical ethics.

4. Hands-On Project: Programming a Robot to Assist with Simple Tasks

In this project, we will design a simple robot capable of performing basic tasks in an urban setting, such as picking up objects, delivering items, or assisting with household chores. This robot will serve as an example of how AI and robotics can be used to improve efficiency and support human activities.

Step 1: Choose the Robot Hardware

For this project, we will use a Raspberry Pi or Arduino-based robot. You will need the following components:

- **Microcontroller** (e.g., Raspberry Pi or Arduino)
- **DC motors** with motor driver shield
- **Ultrasonic sensors** for object detection
- **Servo motors** for grabbing and placing objects
- **Wi-Fi module** (for remote control)
- **Power supply** (e.g., battery pack)

Step 2: Assemble the Robot

Build the robot's chassis, attach the motors and servo, and mount the ultrasonic sensors for obstacle detection. Connect the motors to the motor driver shield and ensure that all components are properly connected to the microcontroller.

Step 3: Write the Code

Program the robot to perform simple tasks. For instance, you can program it to pick up a lightweight object, move to a specified location, and drop it at another spot.

cpp

```cpp
#include <Servo.h>

Servo grabber;

void setup() {
  grabber.attach(9); // Attach the servo to pin 9
  // Initialize motor and sensor pins
```

```
}


void loop() {

    // Use ultrasonic sensor to detect object

    // Move towards object, grab it, and move to
    destination

    grabber.write(90); // Grab object

    delay(1000);

    // Move robot to new location

    grabber.write(0); // Release object

}
```

Step 4: Test the Robot

Run the robot in a controlled environment and test its ability to pick up and move objects. Ensure that the robot responds to the environment, navigates obstacles, and performs tasks as expected.

Step 5: Optimize the Robot

You can optimize the robot by adding more sensors, improving its navigation algorithms, and programming it to respond to different tasks. Experiment with different task types, such as delivering objects to specific locations or assisting with basic household chores.

This hands-on project demonstrates the basics of programming a robot to assist with tasks, laying the foundation for more advanced human-robot interactions. By integrating AI and robotics into urban settings, we can create smarter, more efficient cities that improve quality of life, reduce manual labor, and support a wide range of human activities. Through the principles covered in this chapter and the project, you now have a deeper understanding of how AI and robots can collaborate with humans to shape the cities of the future.

Chapter 12: Smart City Governance and Policy Making

As cities around the world continue to grow, urbanization and technological advancement are creating new opportunities and challenges in governance and policy-making. With the advent of smart cities, which leverage cutting-edge technologies like Artificial Intelligence (AI), Internet of Things (IoT), and data analytics, local governments are able to adopt a more informed, data-driven approach to decision-making. These technologies enable more efficient resource management, enhance the quality of life for residents, and improve overall city operations. However, the integration of AI and data analytics into urban infrastructure raises several legal, ethical, and policy-related issues that must be carefully navigated.

In this chapter, we will explore how AI and data analytics influence urban policy decisions, the crucial role of government and local authorities in the development of smart cities, and the legal and ethical challenges associated with using AI in public infrastructure. Additionally, we will walk through a hands-on project where you will simulate a smart city policy model, allowing you to see how various factors influence decision-making and urban development.

1. How AI and Data Analytics Influence Urban Policy Decisions

AI and data analytics have a transformative impact on the policy-making process in smart cities. Traditionally, city planners and policymakers relied on historical data, manual surveys, and subjective judgment to make decisions. Today, however, AI algorithms and real-time data collection provide a more precise, data-driven approach to urban policy decisions, leading to more effective and efficient governance.

Data-Driven Decision Making

AI and data analytics provide policymakers with valuable insights into city operations, traffic patterns, infrastructure, energy use, and public health. By analyzing vast amounts of data collected from sensors, cameras, social media, and IoT devices, AI can uncover trends, forecast future developments, and offer actionable recommendations. These insights allow policymakers to make more informed decisions that align with the city's needs and goals.

Examples of Data-Driven Urban Policy Decisions:

- **Traffic and Transportation**: AI models can analyze traffic patterns, public transportation usage, and congestion data to develop policies aimed at reducing traffic, optimizing routes, and improving public transit schedules.

- **Urban Planning**: Data analytics help urban planners assess the effectiveness of zoning laws, land use policies, and building codes. By analyzing population density, economic activity, and environmental data, AI can guide decisions on where to build new infrastructure, such as roads, hospitals, schools, and parks.

- **Energy Efficiency**: Smart cities leverage AI to monitor energy consumption in real-time, identify inefficiencies, and optimize energy distribution. AI can recommend policies for reducing energy waste, promoting renewable energy, and ensuring that resources are distributed equitably.

Predictive Analytics for Proactive Policy Making

One of the most powerful uses of AI and data analytics in governance is predictive analytics. By analyzing historical and real-time data, AI can forecast future trends and help governments take proactive measures. This ability to predict potential challenges or opportunities allows policymakers to implement solutions before problems become critical.

Examples of Predictive Analytics in Smart City Policy Making:

- **Public Health**: AI can predict the spread of infectious diseases by analyzing health data, weather patterns, and social factors. This enables governments to take preventive actions, such as deploying resources or implementing lockdown measures, before an outbreak becomes widespread.

- **Crime Prevention**: Predictive policing uses AI to analyze crime data and predict where crimes are likely to occur. This allows law enforcement agencies to allocate resources more effectively, deploy officers to high-risk areas, and prevent criminal activity.

- **Disaster Response**: AI models can predict natural disasters such as floods, earthquakes, or hurricanes based on historical data, weather patterns, and environmental conditions. By using predictive analytics, cities can develop evacuation plans, deploy emergency services, and mitigate the impact of disasters.

Optimizing Urban Services and Infrastructure

AI and data analytics enable cities to optimize urban services and infrastructure by identifying inefficiencies and improving resource allocation. AI can analyze the performance of services such as waste management, water supply, and public transportation, offering insights into where improvements can be made.

Examples of AI Optimization in Urban Services:

- **Smart Waste Management**: AI-powered waste management systems use sensors to monitor waste levels in bins and dumpsters. Data is analyzed to optimize collection routes and schedules, reducing costs and minimizing environmental impact.

- **Water Management**: AI systems can predict water usage patterns and detect leaks in the city's water infrastructure. This helps policymakers develop policies to reduce water waste, manage supply, and improve the sustainability of urban water systems.

- **Energy Management**: AI-powered systems can optimize energy consumption in public buildings, streetlights, and other urban infrastructure. By analyzing usage patterns, these systems can suggest policies to reduce energy waste and promote sustainable energy practices.

2. The Role of Government and Local Authorities in Smart City Development

While technology and data analytics play a crucial role in the development of smart cities, the role of government and local authorities is equally important. Governments are responsible for creating the regulatory framework, funding, and policies that guide the development and implementation of smart city initiatives. Local authorities are tasked with ensuring that these technologies are deployed in ways that benefit all citizens and enhance the overall quality of urban life.

Policy and Regulation for Smart Cities

Governments play a key role in shaping the development of smart cities by establishing policies and regulations that govern the use of technology in urban environments. These policies ensure that technologies are deployed in a way that is safe, ethical, and equitable.

Key Areas of Government Involvement:

- **Data Privacy and Security**: As smart cities collect vast amounts of data, governments must create regulations that ensure the privacy and security of citizens' personal information. Governments must also establish policies on how data is collected, stored, and shared, ensuring that it is used responsibly.

- **Infrastructure Investment**: Governments are responsible for funding the infrastructure needed to support smart city technologies. This includes investments in broadband networks, sensor networks, and data centers that enable IoT and AI systems to function efficiently.

- **Collaboration with Private Sector:** Governments often partner with private companies to develop and implement smart city technologies. These partnerships can help cities access cutting-edge technology and expertise while ensuring that public services are maintained and improved.

Community Engagement and Public Participation

In the development of smart cities, community engagement is vital. Local authorities must ensure that citizens are involved in the planning and decision-making process, especially when it comes to implementing AI-powered systems that may impact daily life.

Approaches to Community Engagement:

- **Public Consultations**: Local authorities can hold public consultations to gather input from residents on proposed smart city initiatives. These consultations allow citizens to voice their concerns, suggest improvements, and ensure that smart city policies reflect the needs of the community.

- **Transparency in Decision-Making**: Governments should ensure that the development of smart cities is transparent and that citizens understand how decisions are made. This includes providing clear information on how data is used, how AI models are developed, and how policies are implemented.

- **Equitable Access**: It is crucial that smart city technologies are accessible to all residents, regardless of income or social status. Governments must implement policies that ensure equitable access to the benefits of smart cities, such as affordable broadband, accessible public transport, and inclusive healthcare services.

Managing Urban Transformation

The development of a smart city involves the transformation of urban spaces, systems, and services. Local authorities must manage this transformation carefully, ensuring that technological advances do not lead to displacement, inequality, or loss of jobs.

Key Considerations for Managing Urban Transformation:

- **Urban Mobility and Accessibility**: Smart city technologies, such as autonomous vehicles and AI-powered public transport systems, should be integrated in a way that improves mobility and accessibility for all citizens. This includes ensuring that transportation systems are affordable, reliable, and accessible to people with disabilities.

- **Job Creation and Skills Development**: The development of smart cities presents both opportunities and challenges for the workforce. Governments must ensure that new technologies create jobs and provide workers with the skills needed to thrive in the digital economy. This may include providing training programs, reskilling initiatives, and supporting the development of tech-based industries.

- **Environmental Sustainability**: Smart cities should be developed with an emphasis on sustainability, reducing waste, energy consumption, and environmental degradation. Governments must implement policies that prioritize green technologies, renewable energy, and sustainable urban planning.

3. Legal and Ethical Challenges of Using AI in Public Infrastructure

As AI and data analytics become more integrated into urban infrastructure, several legal and ethical challenges must be addressed. These challenges revolve around issues such as privacy, bias, accountability, and the ethical use of AI in decision-making processes.

Privacy and Data Protection

One of the primary concerns with the use of AI in smart cities is the collection and storage of personal data. Smart city systems collect vast amounts of data, including information about citizens' movements, preferences, and behaviors. While this data is used to improve city services, there are significant privacy risks if it is not managed properly.

Key Issues:

- **Data Collection and Consent**: Citizens must be informed about what data is being collected and how it will be used. Smart city initiatives should ensure that data is collected transparently and with the consent of individuals.

- **Data Security**: Protecting personal data from cyberattacks is critical. Governments and city planners must ensure that AI systems and data storage platforms have robust security measures in place to prevent breaches and misuse of sensitive information.

- **Anonymization and De-Identification**: To protect privacy, data should be anonymized or de-identified when used for analysis. This ensures that individual identities are not exposed while still allowing cities to benefit from data-driven insights.

Bias and Fairness in AI Systems

AI systems are only as good as the data they are trained on. If AI models are trained on biased data, they can make decisions that disproportionately affect certain groups of people. In smart cities, this could lead to inequities in services like policing, healthcare, or housing.

Key Issues:

- **Algorithmic Bias**: AI algorithms must be tested and audited to ensure they do not perpetuate or exacerbate biases based on race, gender, socio-economic status, or other factors. Governments must ensure that AI systems used in public infrastructure are fair and transparent.

- **Discrimination in Service Delivery**: AI models that influence public services, such as housing allocation, job matching, or credit scoring, must be carefully managed to avoid discrimination. Governments must ensure that these systems are regularly audited for fairness.

Accountability and Liability

As AI systems become more autonomous, questions about accountability arise. If an AI system makes a mistake or causes harm, who is responsible? Is it the developer, the government, or the AI itself?

Key Issues:

- **Liability for AI Decisions**: Governments and regulatory bodies must establish clear guidelines for accountability in the event that an AI system causes harm or makes a decision that results in negative consequences.

- **Transparency in Decision-Making**: It is important that AI systems used in public infrastructure are explainable. Citizens must understand how decisions are being made, particularly when those decisions impact their daily lives.

4. Hands-On Project: Simulating a Smart City Policy Model

In this hands-on project, you will simulate a smart city policy model using AI and data analytics. This simulation will allow you to explore how different factors, such as urban growth, resource management, and transportation policies, influence decision-making in a smart city environment.

Step 1: Choose the Parameters

First, define the parameters of your simulation. Decide which aspects of the smart city you want to focus on, such as transportation, energy consumption, waste management, or public health. Select key factors that will influence the policies, such as population growth, technological advancements, and environmental sustainability.

Step 2: Collect and Analyze Data

Gather data on the chosen parameters. This could include population demographics, traffic patterns, resource usage, or environmental data. Use data analytics tools to process and analyze the data, identifying trends and potential areas for policy intervention.

Step 3: Develop Policy Scenarios

Create different policy scenarios based on the data analysis. For example, you could simulate the impact of introducing autonomous vehicles on traffic congestion, or the effect of implementing a smart grid on energy consumption. Consider how each policy might impact citizens, the economy, and the environment.

Step 4: Run the Simulation

Use AI algorithms to run the simulation, analyzing the potential outcomes of each policy scenario. Track the results in real-time and assess the impact of different variables, such as changes in technology, infrastructure, or governance.

Step 5: Evaluate and Present Findings

Evaluate the outcomes of the simulation and present your findings. Identify which policies are most effective in addressing urban challenges and promoting sustainable development. Provide recommendations for improving the smart city model and addressing any issues that arose during the simulation.

This project demonstrates how AI and data analytics can be used to simulate urban policies and decision-making processes. By integrating these technologies, city planners and policymakers can make more informed, data-driven decisions that benefit all citizens, enhance urban efficiency, and promote sustainability. Through this hands-on experience, you will gain a deeper understanding of the complexities involved in smart city governance and policy-making.

Chapter 13: Building Smart City Solutions with AI and IoT

As cities around the world continue to grow, the integration of Artificial Intelligence (AI) and the Internet of Things (IoT) offers unprecedented opportunities to solve some of the most pressing urban challenges. From traffic congestion and waste management to energy efficiency and public health, smart cities are harnessing the power of AI and IoT to create more sustainable, efficient, and livable urban environments. The convergence of these technologies is reshaping the way cities function and interact with their inhabitants.

This chapter will explore how AI and IoT are being used to build solutions for urban challenges. We'll look at the process of designing and implementing these solutions, the collaborative efforts needed between urban planners, local governments, and technology developers, and the tools and platforms that enable the creation of smart city systems. Additionally, we'll walk through a hands-on project to build a smart waste management system, giving you practical experience in creating a solution that tackles one of the most critical challenges of modern urban life.

1. Designing and Implementing AI and IoT Solutions for Urban Challenges

Urban challenges are complex, often involving multiple stakeholders and requiring sophisticated technologies to address them effectively. AI and IoT provide powerful tools for monitoring, analyzing, and managing city infrastructure and services. These technologies enable cities to collect real-time data, identify patterns, and make data-driven decisions that improve urban life.

Urban Challenges Addressed by AI and IoT

Cities face a range of challenges, many of which can be addressed by AI and IoT. Some of the most significant challenges include:

- **Traffic and Transportation**: With growing populations and increasing car ownership, urban congestion is a significant issue. AI and IoT can help by optimizing traffic flow, improving public transportation systems, and promoting the use of autonomous vehicles.

- **Waste Management**: As urban populations grow, the volume of waste produced by cities increases. Traditional waste management systems are often inefficient and costly. Smart waste management systems, powered by IoT sensors and AI algorithms, can optimize waste collection, reduce operational costs, and improve recycling efforts.

- **Energy Efficiency**: Cities are large consumers of energy, and inefficient energy use can result in increased costs and environmental impact. AI-powered smart grids and energy management systems can optimize energy distribution, reduce waste, and integrate renewable energy sources.

- **Water Management**: Managing urban water systems efficiently is critical for ensuring sustainable water use, preventing shortages, and maintaining infrastructure. IoT sensors can monitor water usage, detect leaks, and optimize water distribution systems, while AI can forecast demand and improve resource allocation.

- **Public Health and Safety**: Monitoring air quality, predicting disease outbreaks, and improving emergency response times are essential components of urban health and safety. AI and IoT can help by providing real-time data on environmental conditions, tracking health metrics, and predicting public health trends.

The Design Process for Smart City Solutions

Designing a smart city solution involves understanding the problem, selecting the right technology, and creating a system that can be deployed and scaled effectively. The process typically follows these steps:

1. **Identifying the Problem**: The first step in designing a smart city solution is identifying the specific urban challenge that needs to be addressed. Whether it's traffic congestion, waste management, or energy efficiency, the

problem must be clearly defined so that the right technology can be applied.

2. **Data Collection**: AI and IoT solutions rely heavily on data. Sensors, devices, and other IoT technologies collect data from the city's infrastructure, environment, and citizens. This data serves as the foundation for decision-making and the development of AI algorithms that drive smart city solutions.

3. **Designing the Solution**: Once the problem and data have been identified, the next step is to design a solution that uses AI and IoT to address the challenge. This may involve developing custom algorithms, integrating sensors, or creating a communication platform that connects all of the devices and systems.

4. **Implementation**: After the solution has been designed, it must be implemented in the real world. This involves setting up IoT sensors, installing devices, and deploying AI algorithms across the city's infrastructure. The implementation phase also includes testing the solution, gathering feedback, and making necessary adjustments.

5. **Optimization and Scaling**: Once the solution is live, continuous optimization is necessary to ensure that it is working as efficiently as possible. AI models must be regularly trained on new data to improve accuracy, and the system must be scaled to handle more data and more complex scenarios as the city grows.

2. Collaborative Projects: Working with Urban Planners and Local Governments

Building smart city solutions requires collaboration between a wide range of stakeholders, including urban planners, local governments, technology developers, and the citizens who will benefit from these solutions. Each of these stakeholders plays a unique role in ensuring that smart city initiatives are successful and that they address the needs of the entire community.

The Role of Urban Planners

Urban planners are responsible for designing and organizing the physical layout of cities. They focus on how land is used, the placement of infrastructure, transportation systems, and the overall design of urban environments. When working on smart city projects, urban planners must consider how technology can be integrated into existing infrastructure and how new technologies will affect the city's development.

Key Contributions of Urban Planners:

- **Zoning and Land Use**: Urban planners help determine where smart infrastructure, such as sensors and data collection devices, should be deployed. They ensure that technology is integrated into the urban fabric without disrupting existing systems.

- **Sustainability Goals**: Urban planners often work with city governments to create sustainable development goals. They use AI and IoT to help design energy-efficient buildings, optimize waste management, and promote green spaces in urban environments.

- **Public Spaces and Accessibility**: Urban planners ensure that public spaces are designed in a way that is accessible to all citizens. They use technology to create inclusive, user-friendly spaces and ensure that smart systems are accessible to people with disabilities.

Local governments are responsible for the implementation and regulation of policies that govern smart city projects. They provide the funding, oversight, and regulatory framework that guide the development of AI and IoT solutions. Local governments also play a key role in engaging with citizens and ensuring that technology is used in ways that benefit everyone in the community.

Key Contributions of Local Governments:

- **Policy and Regulation**: Local governments are responsible for creating the regulatory framework that governs smart city projects. This includes setting policies for data privacy, security, and ethical AI use, as well as ensuring that the technology is accessible and beneficial to all citizens.

- **Funding and Investment**: Local governments provide funding for smart city projects, whether through public-private partnerships, grants, or other financial mechanisms. They also help prioritize which projects should be funded based on their potential impact on urban life.

- **Public Engagement**: Local governments work with citizens to ensure that smart city solutions meet their needs. This includes engaging the public in decision-making, conducting consultations, and providing information about how technology will be used in the city.

Public-Private Partnerships

Smart city solutions often involve collaboration between public and private sector stakeholders. Technology companies bring expertise in AI, IoT, and data analytics, while public sector organizations provide the regulatory framework and funding necessary to scale solutions. These partnerships are critical for creating sustainable, effective smart cities.

3. Tools and Platforms for Building Smart City Solutions

Building smart city solutions requires the right set of tools and platforms to collect data, analyze it, and deploy AI-driven technologies. These tools and platforms help cities integrate various systems, automate processes, and provide real-time insights into urban operations.

IoT platforms provide the foundation for building and managing smart city systems. These platforms connect IoT devices, sensors, and other technologies, allowing cities to collect and analyze data in real time.

Examples of IoT Platforms for Smart Cities:

- **ThingSpeak**: ThingSpeak is an open-source IoT platform that allows cities to collect, analyze, and visualize data from sensors in real-time. It is widely used for applications like traffic monitoring, environmental sensing, and energy management.

- **Cisco Kinetic**: Cisco Kinetic is an IoT platform designed to help cities manage and analyze data from connected devices. It supports applications in transportation, waste management, and public safety.

- **Microsoft Azure IoT**: Microsoft Azure IoT provides a comprehensive suite of services for connecting IoT devices and managing smart city infrastructure. It enables cities to collect data, analyze it using AI models, and scale solutions across urban environments.

AI and Machine Learning Tools

AI and machine learning are essential for analyzing the vast amounts of data generated by IoT devices. These tools enable cities to make data-driven decisions, optimize operations, and create predictive models for urban planning.

Examples of AI Tools for Smart Cities:

- **Google Cloud AI**: Google Cloud provides AI tools and machine learning models that can be used for a variety of smart city applications, including traffic management, energy optimization, and public safety.

- **IBM Watson for Cities**: IBM Watson provides AI-powered tools for cities to analyze data and improve urban operations. It offers solutions for traffic management, waste reduction, and predictive maintenance.

- **TensorFlow**: TensorFlow, an open-source machine learning framework, is widely used to develop AI models for smart city applications. Cities can use TensorFlow to create predictive models for traffic patterns, energy consumption, and even disaster response.

Data analytics and visualization platforms help cities make sense of the large volumes of data generated by IoT devices. These platforms enable city officials to monitor performance, identify trends, and make informed decisions.

Examples of Data Analytics Tools for Smart Cities:

- **Tableau**: Tableau is a data visualization tool that allows cities to create interactive dashboards and reports based on data collected from IoT devices. It is commonly used for traffic monitoring, energy usage analysis, and citizen engagement.

- **Power BI**: Microsoft's Power BI is another data visualization tool that integrates with IoT platforms to provide real-time insights into urban operations. Cities can use Power BI to track performance metrics, analyze trends, and make data-driven decisions.

- **Qlik**: Qlik is a business intelligence tool that enables cities to create interactive dashboards, visualize trends, and optimize operations. It is particularly useful for monitoring public services, transportation, and energy efficiency.

4. Hands-On Project: Building a Smart Waste Management System

In this project, we will build a simple smart waste management system using IoT sensors and AI algorithms. The goal is to design a system that can monitor waste levels in bins, optimize collection schedules, and provide real-time data for urban waste management.

Step 1: Set Up the Hardware

For this project, you will need the following components:

- **Microcontroller** (e.g., Arduino or Raspberry Pi)

- **Ultrasonic sensors** to measure the fill levels in waste bins

- **Wi-Fi module** (e.g., ESP8266) for cloud connectivity

- **Relay module** for controlling waste collection systems

- **Power supply** (e.g., battery pack)

Step 2: Connect the Sensors

Connect the ultrasonic sensors to the microcontroller to measure the fill levels of waste bins. The sensors will send distance readings to the microcontroller, which will be used to determine if the bin is full and when it needs to be collected.

Step 3: Set Up the Cloud Platform

Set up a cloud platform, such as ThingSpeak or Blynk, to collect and analyze data from the waste bins. This platform will store the fill levels of the bins and allow city managers to monitor the status of the bins in real-time.

Step 4: Write the Code

Write a program to monitor the distance readings from the ultrasonic sensors and send the data to the cloud platform. If the bin is full, the system will send an alert to the waste management team to collect the waste.

cpp

```cpp
#include <ThingSpeak.h>
```

```
#include <ESP8266WiFi.h>

const int ultrasonicTrigPin = D1;
const int ultrasonicEchoPin = D2;

WiFiClient client;

void setup() {
  pinMode(ultrasonicTrigPin, OUTPUT);
  pinMode(ultrasonicEchoPin, INPUT);
  WiFi.begin("yourSSID", "yourPassword");
  ThingSpeak.begin(client);
}

void loop() {
  long duration, distance;
  digitalWrite(ultrasonicTrigPin, LOW);
  delayMicroseconds(2);
```

```
digitalWrite(ultrasonicTrigPin, HIGH);

delayMicroseconds(10);

digitalWrite(ultrasonicTrigPin, LOW);

duration = pulseIn(ultrasonicEchoPin, HIGH);

distance = duration * 0.034 / 2;


ThingSpeak.setField(1, distance);

ThingSpeak.writeFields(yourChannelID,
"yourWriteAPIKey");


if (distance < 10) { // Bin is full

  // Send an alert for waste collection

  ThingSpeak.setField(2, 1); // Alert flag

}


delay(60000); // Wait 1 minute before checking again

}
```

Step 5: Test the System

Once the system is set up, test it by placing the ultrasonic sensors in waste bins and monitoring the fill levels. Verify that the system sends data to the cloud and triggers alerts when bins are full.

Step 6: Optimize the System

You can optimize the system by adding more sensors, improving the data analysis algorithms, and integrating the system with a waste collection scheduling platform. This will allow the city to optimize waste collection routes and schedules, reducing operational costs and environmental impact.

This project demonstrates how AI and IoT can be used to solve urban challenges, such as waste management. By collecting data from IoT sensors and analyzing it with AI algorithms, cities can optimize operations, reduce waste, and improve overall urban efficiency. Through this project and the concepts explored in this chapter, you have gained practical experience in designing and implementing smart city solutions that tackle real-world urban problems.

Chapter 14: Challenges and Solutions in Smart City Development

The evolution of smart cities presents a remarkable opportunity to transform urban environments into more efficient, sustainable, and livable spaces. With the integration of Artificial Intelligence (AI), Internet of Things (IoT), and other cutting-edge technologies, cities can optimize resource use, reduce energy consumption, improve public safety, and provide better services to residents. However, building smart cities is not without its challenges. The development of these cities involves complex technological, social, and economic considerations that must be addressed to ensure their success.

This chapter explores the key challenges in smart city development, including technological barriers, social and economic obstacles, and issues surrounding data privacy, security, and ethics. It also examines the strategies and solutions available to overcome these hurdles. Finally, we will walk through a hands-on project where you will develop a risk management plan for a smart city initiative, equipping you with the skills to identify potential risks and devise strategies to mitigate them effectively.

1. Technological, Social, and Economic Challenges of Building Smart Cities

While the promise of smart cities is vast, the path to creating them is filled with obstacles. These obstacles can be broadly categorized into technological challenges, social issues, and economic barriers.

Technological Challenges

The rapid pace of technological change is both a benefit and a challenge in the development of smart cities. New technologies emerge regularly, and integrating them into existing urban systems requires significant investment, coordination, and expertise.

Key Technological Challenges:

1. **Interoperability of Systems**: One of the most pressing technological challenges in smart city development is ensuring that the various systems and platforms work together seamlessly. A smart city is composed of many different technologies—traffic management systems, energy grids, water networks, healthcare platforms, and more. These systems must be able to communicate with each other, share data, and collaborate in real time. Ensuring interoperability is critical for ensuring that all systems work together to deliver a cohesive, efficient urban environment.

2. **Data Management and Integration**: Smart cities generate massive amounts of data from sensors, IoT devices, and other sources. Managing, storing, and analyzing this data is a significant challenge. Cities need robust infrastructure to process and analyze this data in real time, and the platforms used to collect and store this data must be scalable to handle large volumes of information. Effective data integration, ensuring that data from various

systems can be combined and utilized, is also crucial for developing insights and making informed decisions.

3. **Infrastructure and Legacy Systems**: Many cities have existing infrastructure—roads, bridges, utilities—that were not designed to accommodate modern smart technologies. Retrofitting existing infrastructure to support IoT devices, sensors, and AI algorithms can be expensive and logistically challenging. Additionally, legacy systems may be outdated, incompatible with new technologies, and require significant upgrades to function in a smart city environment.

4. **Connectivity and Network Infrastructure**: Building a reliable and fast network infrastructure to support IoT devices and data transmission is a major hurdle. Many smart city applications rely on continuous, high-speed data transfers, which requires a robust internet backbone. In some regions, particularly in developing countries, poor connectivity can impede the deployment of smart city technologies. Expanding high-speed broadband

and 5G networks is essential to ensuring that smart city systems work efficiently.

Social Challenges

Smart cities are designed to enhance quality of life and provide a better living environment for citizens, but the implementation of these technologies can also create social challenges.

Key Social Challenges:

1. **Digital Divide**: While smart cities aim to provide better services for all citizens, there is a risk that certain groups may be left behind. People without access to technology or the skills to use digital services may be excluded from the benefits of smart cities. This digital divide can exacerbate social inequality and create disparities in access to services like healthcare, transportation, and education.

2. **Public Acceptance and Trust**: The success of smart cities depends on public trust and acceptance of the technologies being implemented. If citizens feel that their privacy is being compromised or that the technologies are too intrusive, they may resist the adoption of

smart city solutions. Transparency about how data is used and how AI systems make decisions is crucial to gaining public support.

3. **Job Displacement and Workforce Transition**: The automation enabled by AI and IoT systems in smart cities can lead to job displacement in certain sectors. For example, the widespread adoption of autonomous vehicles may reduce the need for truck drivers and taxi drivers. Cities must plan for workforce transitions and provide reskilling opportunities to ensure that displaced workers can find new jobs in the evolving economy.

4. **Ethical Concerns in Decision-Making**: As AI and data-driven technologies become more integrated into urban governance, questions arise about who is making decisions and how ethical considerations are handled. For example, AI systems used in policing or healthcare may inadvertently reinforce biases or make decisions that are unfair or discriminatory. Addressing these concerns is vital to ensuring that smart city technologies benefit all citizens equitably.

Economic Challenges

While the benefits of smart cities are substantial, the economic cost of building and maintaining these systems can be prohibitive, particularly for smaller municipalities or developing nations.

Key Economic Challenges:

1. **High Initial Investment**: Building a smart city infrastructure requires significant upfront investment in technology, infrastructure, and human resources. Cities need to invest in IoT sensors, data centers, high-speed connectivity, and AI systems. The costs of retrofitting existing infrastructure and ensuring that technologies are scalable further add to the economic burden.

2. **Sustainability and Long-Term Funding**: The financial sustainability of smart city projects is a major concern. While the initial costs can be high, cities must also ensure that they have the resources to maintain and upgrade the technologies over time. Long-term funding models, such as public-private partnerships (PPPs), are essential to sustaining smart city

projects and ensuring that they deliver ongoing value to residents.

3. **Economic Disparities**: Smart city development can disproportionately benefit wealthy neighborhoods and urban centers, while poorer regions may struggle to access the same services. Ensuring that smart city solutions are accessible and beneficial to all citizens requires careful economic planning, including equitable distribution of resources and services.

2. Addressing Data Privacy, Security, and Ethical Issues

With the increasing collection of data from citizens, smart cities face significant challenges related to data privacy, security, and ethics. These issues must be addressed to ensure that smart city technologies do not compromise personal freedoms or result in unintended consequences.

Data Privacy

As cities become more connected, they collect vast amounts of data about their citizens. This data includes personal information such as health records, transportation patterns, and spending habits.

Ensuring the privacy of this data is crucial to maintaining public trust.

Key Issues:

- **Surveillance and Data Collection**: Cities need to balance the benefits of data collection with the right to privacy. Excessive surveillance through cameras, sensors, and tracking systems can be seen as invasive, particularly if the data is used for purposes other than what was originally intended. Policies must be in place to ensure that citizens' privacy is respected and that data collection is done transparently.

- **Data Ownership and Consent**: Citizens must be informed about what data is being collected and how it will be used. Data ownership is another issue—should individuals have control over their personal data, or should cities and governments own the data collected by smart city systems?

- **Data Sharing and Third-Party Use**: Many smart city systems rely on sharing data across various platforms and with third parties. Ensuring that data sharing is done responsibly, and that third parties adhere to data protection standards, is essential to preventing misuse or unauthorized access.

Data Security

Data security is a critical concern for smart cities, particularly because a breach in a city's infrastructure could have catastrophic consequences. From unauthorized access to hacking attacks, cities must implement robust cybersecurity measures to protect sensitive data and ensure the safe operation of critical systems.

Key Issues:

- **Cybersecurity Threats**: As cities rely on interconnected IoT devices and AI systems, they become more vulnerable to cyberattacks. Smart city infrastructure must be protected from malicious actors who may seek to disrupt services, steal data, or compromise public safety.

- **Data Encryption and Storage**: Ensuring that data is securely stored and transmitted is essential to protecting citizens' privacy. Cities must use encryption techniques and secure storage solutions to safeguard personal and sensitive information.

Ethical Issues in Smart City Technologies

The use of AI in smart cities raises important ethical questions about fairness, transparency, and accountability. As AI systems make decisions that affect citizens, it is essential to ensure that these systems operate in ways that are ethical and unbiased.

Key Issues:

- **Algorithmic Bias**: AI systems are only as good as the data they are trained on. If the data used to train AI models is biased, the system's decisions will also be biased. This could result in discriminatory outcomes in areas like policing, healthcare, and hiring. Ensuring that AI systems are fair and unbiased is crucial to building trust and ensuring that smart cities benefit all citizens equally.

- **Decision-Making Transparency**: AI-driven decisions in smart cities must be transparent. Citizens must understand how decisions are being made, particularly when those decisions impact their lives. For example, if AI is used to allocate resources or determine eligibility for services, the criteria and process behind those decisions should be clear and open.

- **Accountability for AI Decisions**: As AI systems take on more responsibility in city governance, questions of accountability arise. If an AI system makes a decision that leads to harm or injustice, who is responsible? Should the city, the technology provider, or the AI system itself be held accountable?

3. Overcoming Public Resistance to AI and Automation

Despite the benefits of AI and automation in smart cities, public resistance remains one of the biggest barriers to their adoption. People often fear the unknown, and there are concerns about job displacement, privacy violations, and loss of control.

Key Strategies for Overcoming Resistance:

1. **Public Education and Awareness**: Educating the public about the benefits of AI and automation is crucial for overcoming

resistance. Cities should engage with citizens, provide information about how AI and automation work, and highlight the positive impact these technologies can have on their lives.

2. **Transparency and Inclusivity**: Governments and technology providers should be transparent about how AI systems are being used and how data is being collected and stored. Public consultations and inclusive decision-making processes can help ensure that citizens feel involved and their concerns are addressed.

3. **Job Transition Programs**: To address fears of job displacement, cities can implement programs that help workers transition to new roles. Reskilling and upskilling initiatives, as well as support for entrepreneurship, can help ensure that people are prepared for the changing job market.

4. **Human-Centered Design**: When designing AI and automation systems, cities must prioritize human needs and ensure that these technologies are designed to complement, rather than replace, human workers. Human-

centered design principles ensure that technology enhances human capabilities and improves the quality of life for residents.

4. Hands-On Project: Developing a Risk Management Plan for a Smart City Initiative

In this project, you will develop a risk management plan for a smart city initiative. The goal is to identify potential risks, assess their impact, and create strategies to mitigate them. This exercise will help you understand the importance of risk management in the successful deployment of smart city technologies.

Step 1: Identify the Smart City Initiative

Choose a specific smart city initiative to focus on, such as smart waste management, smart traffic systems, or public health monitoring. Define the objectives and scope of the project, and identify the stakeholders involved.

Step 2: Conduct a Risk Assessment

Identify potential risks that could impact the success of the initiative. These could include technological risks (e.g., system failure, cybersecurity breaches), social risks (e.g., public resistance, job displacement), and legal risks (e.g., data privacy violations, regulatory non-compliance). Assess the likelihood and impact of each risk.

Step 3: Develop Mitigation Strategies

For each identified risk, develop mitigation strategies to reduce or eliminate its impact. This could involve implementing backup systems, ensuring data security, engaging with the public to build trust, or creating legal frameworks to address privacy concerns.

Step 4: Create a Contingency Plan

Develop a contingency plan that outlines the steps to take if a risk materializes. This plan should include clear procedures for responding to issues, communicating with stakeholders, and minimizing damage.

Step 5: Monitor and Review

Once the risk management plan is in place, establish mechanisms for monitoring and reviewing the plan's effectiveness. This could include regular audits, feedback loops with citizens, and the use of AI models to predict and mitigate new risks as the project progresses.

This hands-on project provides you with a comprehensive understanding of how to manage risks in smart city initiatives. By identifying potential risks and developing strategies to address them, you can ensure that smart city projects are successful, sustainable, and beneficial to all residents. Through this chapter, you've gained a deeper understanding of the challenges and solutions in building smart cities, and the skills to navigate these complexities in the real world.

Chapter 15: The Future of Smart Cities: Trends and Innovations

The concept of smart cities has rapidly evolved over the past decade, moving from theoretical discussions to tangible projects in cities across the world. These cities leverage emerging technologies to enhance the quality of urban life, optimize infrastructure, and make public services more efficient. The next phase of smart city development promises to be even more transformative as new technologies such as 5G, blockchain, and edge computing come into play. Furthermore, AI continues to evolve, becoming an even more integral part of urban development. The future of smart cities will not only focus on technological advancements but also how these innovations reshape the way we live, work, and interact within urban environments.

In this chapter, we will explore emerging technologies driving the future of smart cities, the evolving role of AI in urban development, and how these innovations are shaping the future of urban living. Additionally, we will undertake a hands-on project where you will design a prototype for a future smart city, considering the latest trends and the integration of cutting-edge technologies.

1. Emerging Technologies: 5G, Blockchain, and Edge Computing

As cities adopt smarter technologies, the demand for faster, more secure, and decentralized solutions grows. The next generation of urban innovation is heavily reliant on advancements in communication, computation, and data security. Three key technologies stand out as game-changers in the smart city ecosystem: **5G**, **blockchain**, and **edge computing**.

5G: The Backbone of Smart City Connectivity

The rollout of 5G networks represents a significant leap in communication infrastructure. This next-generation cellular technology promises faster data speeds, lower latency, and more reliable connections. 5G will serve as the backbone for many smart city applications by providing the high-speed connectivity required for IoT devices, autonomous vehicles, smart grids, and real-time data analysis.

- **Faster Data Speeds**: 5G can deliver download speeds up to 100 times faster than 4G, allowing cities to collect and process vast amounts of data in real-time. This enables smart city applications like traffic management, emergency response, and public health monitoring to function more effectively.

- **Lower Latency**: The reduced latency (delay) offered by 5G means that data can be transmitted with minimal delay. This is critical for applications that require instantaneous responses, such as autonomous vehicle navigation or remote surgery. Real-time decision-making becomes feasible, leading to more efficient urban systems.

- **Greater Device Density**: 5G can support millions of devices per square kilometer, making it ideal for IoT-heavy environments. With the proliferation of sensors, cameras, and smart devices in cities, 5G's ability to handle high device density is crucial for scalable smart city solutions.

Example: Smart Traffic Management with 5G

In cities like Singapore, smart traffic management systems are leveraging 5G to provide real-time traffic data and allow vehicles to communicate with each other. By analyzing traffic patterns and integrating data from road sensors, AI algorithms can adjust traffic lights in real-time, improving the flow of traffic and reducing congestion. The low latency of 5G enables this data processing to occur almost instantaneously, ensuring a smoother commute for citizens.

Blockchain: Securing Data and Enhancing Transparency

Blockchain technology, best known as the foundation of cryptocurrencies like Bitcoin, is increasingly being explored for its potential in enhancing security, transparency, and efficiency in smart city applications. At its core, blockchain is a decentralized, distributed ledger that records transactions across multiple computers, ensuring that the data is tamper-proof and transparent.

- **Data Integrity:** Blockchain's immutable nature ensures that once data is recorded, it cannot be altered without detection. This makes it an excellent solution for maintaining the integrity of urban data, such as traffic information, financial transactions, and public service records.

- **Decentralized Identity and Access Management:** Blockchain can also be used to create secure, decentralized digital identities for residents. By utilizing blockchain, cities can provide secure access to services such as healthcare, voting, and public transportation without relying on centralized databases that are vulnerable to hacking or data breaches.

- **Smart Contracts:** Smart contracts are self-executing contracts with the terms of the agreement directly written into code. These contracts can automatically execute actions such as releasing funds or initiating service deliveries when predetermined conditions are met, improving efficiency and reducing administrative overhead.

Example: Blockchain for Secure Voting

In a smart city, blockchain can be used to enable secure, transparent voting systems for local elections or civic engagement. Blockchain ensures that each vote is securely recorded and cannot be tampered with, providing an immutable audit trail that enhances trust in the electoral process.

Edge Computing: Decentralizing Data Processing

Edge computing involves processing data closer to the source of data generation rather than relying on a centralized cloud server. By moving computation to the "edge" of the network, where devices and sensors are located, edge computing helps to reduce latency, save bandwidth, and enable real-time decision-making.

- **Faster Response Times**: By processing data locally, edge computing enables faster decision-making, which is critical for time-sensitive smart city applications such as autonomous vehicles, public safety systems, and traffic management.

- **Bandwidth Efficiency**: Smart cities generate enormous volumes of data from IoT devices.

Sending all of this data to centralized cloud servers can strain network bandwidth and increase operational costs. Edge computing allows for the filtration and preprocessing of data locally, sending only relevant data to the cloud for further analysis.

- **Resilience and Reliability**: Edge computing enhances the resilience of smart city systems by enabling devices to continue functioning even if connectivity to the cloud is disrupted. Local processing ensures that essential services, such as traffic lights or emergency systems, remain operational.

Example: Edge Computing in Autonomous Vehicles

Autonomous vehicles rely heavily on real-time data processing to navigate safely and efficiently. By using edge computing, vehicles can process data from sensors, cameras, and LiDAR locally, enabling immediate decision-making for tasks like obstacle avoidance and route optimization. This minimizes the risk of delays that could occur if the data had to be sent to a central server for processing.

2. The Evolving Role of AI in Urban Development

Artificial Intelligence is poised to play an even larger role in the future of smart cities, driving innovation in urban planning, transportation, energy management, healthcare, and more. AI's ability to analyze large datasets, learn from patterns, and make real-time decisions makes it a crucial component of modern urban development.

AI in Urban Planning and Infrastructure

AI can transform the way cities are planned and built. By analyzing historical data, traffic patterns, population growth, and environmental factors, AI can assist urban planners in designing more sustainable and efficient cities. AI-powered predictive models can simulate how urban environments will evolve over time, helping planners anticipate needs for housing, transportation, and green spaces.

- **Smart Zoning and Land Use**: AI can analyze various data points, such as population density, traffic flow, and proximity to amenities, to recommend optimal land use and zoning strategies. This ensures that cities are developed in ways that maximize efficiency, minimize congestion, and meet the needs of growing populations.

- **Urban Heat Island Effect**: Cities tend to trap heat, creating "urban heat islands" that raise local temperatures. AI can model temperature variations across a city and recommend solutions such as green roofs, urban parks, or reflective building materials to mitigate this effect.

AI in Public Safety and Law Enforcement

AI has the potential to greatly enhance public safety in smart cities. Through the use of machine learning, computer vision, and predictive analytics, AI systems can detect anomalies, predict criminal activity, and assist in emergency response.

- **Predictive Policing**: AI systems can analyze crime data to identify patterns and predict where and when crimes are likely to occur. This enables law enforcement agencies to allocate resources more efficiently, focusing on areas at high risk of criminal activity.

- **Facial Recognition and Surveillance**: AI-powered facial recognition systems can be used to enhance security in public spaces. These systems can identify individuals of interest, track movements, and assist in locating missing persons or apprehending suspects. However, this raises significant privacy concerns, which must be addressed through regulation and transparency.

AI in Environmental Sustainability

AI will play a crucial role in creating more sustainable urban environments. By leveraging AI, cities can optimize energy consumption, reduce waste, and promote environmental conservation.

- **Energy Management**: AI can analyze energy usage patterns and recommend ways to optimize energy consumption in smart buildings, streetlights, and public transportation systems. For example, AI can automatically adjust lighting and heating based on occupancy patterns, ensuring that energy is used efficiently.

- **Waste Reduction**: AI-powered systems can predict waste generation patterns, helping cities optimize waste collection routes and schedules. Additionally, AI can assist in recycling by identifying recyclable materials and sorting waste more effectively.

AI in Healthcare and Public Health

AI's potential in healthcare extends beyond improving individual health outcomes. In smart cities, AI can be used to monitor public health trends, predict disease outbreaks, and manage healthcare resources more efficiently.

- **Epidemic Prediction**: By analyzing data from hospitals, public health agencies, and social media, AI can help predict and track the spread of infectious diseases. This allows governments to respond proactively, allocating medical resources and implementing preventive measures before an outbreak becomes widespread.

- **Personalized Healthcare**: AI can analyze patient data to provide personalized treatment recommendations and predict health risks. In smart cities, AI-powered healthcare systems can offer real-time health monitoring through wearable devices and provide alerts when interventions are needed.

3. How Smart Cities Are Shaping the Future of Urban Living

The advancements in technology are not just transforming how cities operate—they are also reshaping how we live in urban environments. Smart cities promise to improve the quality of life for their residents by providing more efficient services, enhancing sustainability, and fostering social well-being.

Enhanced Mobility and Transportation

Smart cities will provide citizens with a range of transportation options that are efficient, safe, and environmentally friendly. With the integration of autonomous vehicles, electric cars, and shared mobility platforms, commuting will become more convenient and less polluting.

- **Multi-Modal Transportation Systems**: Smart cities will offer integrated transportation systems where citizens can seamlessly switch between modes of transport—such as electric scooters, buses, trains, and autonomous vehicles—based on real-time data and personal preferences. AI will play a critical role in optimizing routes and schedules to reduce congestion and improve efficiency.

- **Electric and Autonomous Vehicles**: With the growing adoption of electric vehicles (EVs) and autonomous vehicles (AVs), cities will experience a reduction in carbon emissions, improved traffic flow, and increased safety. AI-powered systems will optimize the charging of EVs and manage the movement of AVs to ensure smooth and efficient transportation.

Sustainable Urban Living

The future of smart cities will be defined by sustainability. By optimizing resource usage, reducing waste, and promoting green energy, smart cities will become more eco-friendly and resilient.

- **Green Buildings and Infrastructure**: Smart buildings will be energy-efficient, equipped with sensors and AI systems to manage lighting, heating, and cooling. Cities will also prioritize green spaces and nature-based solutions to improve air quality, reduce the urban heat island effect, and increase biodiversity.

- **Circular Economy and Waste Management**: A circular economy, where resources are reused and waste is minimized, will be a hallmark of smart cities. Through smart waste management systems, cities will recycle more materials, reduce landfill waste, and promote sustainability through AI and IoT solutions.

Citizen Engagement and Empowerment

In the future, citizens will play a more active role in shaping the development of their cities. Smart city technologies will empower residents by providing them with the tools to engage with local governments, access services, and participate in decision-making.

- **Digital Platforms for Civic Engagement**: Smart cities will use digital platforms to facilitate communication between residents and local authorities. Citizens will be able to report issues, provide feedback, and participate in decision-making processes through mobile apps, online portals, and social media.

- **Smart Healthcare and Education**: AI-powered systems will enable personalized education and healthcare, ensuring that citizens receive the services they need when they need them. By integrating technology into these sectors, smart cities will promote well-being, reduce inequalities, and ensure access to essential services.

4. Hands-On Project: Designing a Future Smart City Prototype

In this project, you will design a prototype for a future smart city, incorporating emerging technologies like 5G, blockchain, edge computing, and AI. The goal is to create a conceptual model of a city that addresses current urban challenges while leveraging these technologies to improve the quality of life for residents.

Step 1: Define the Scope and Objectives

Start by identifying the key urban challenges that your smart city prototype will address. These could include traffic congestion, waste management, energy efficiency, public health, or social equity. Define the objectives of your smart city—how will technology solve these problems and improve urban life?

Step 2: Select Emerging Technologies

Choose the emerging technologies that will drive the development of your smart city. Consider integrating

5G for high-speed connectivity, blockchain for secure data management, and edge computing for real-time decision-making. Use AI for predictive analytics, smart transportation, and resource optimization.

Step 3: Design Key Systems and Infrastructure

Design the key systems and infrastructure that will make your smart city functional. These could include:

- **Smart transportation systems** that use AI and 5G to optimize traffic and integrate autonomous vehicles.

- **Smart waste management** using IoT sensors and AI to optimize collection routes and recycling efforts.

- **Smart energy grids** that use blockchain for secure transactions and edge computing to optimize energy distribution.

Step 4: Create a Citizen-Centric Plan

Ensure that your smart city prototype focuses on enhancing the quality of life for residents. Design systems that empower citizens through digital platforms, personalized healthcare, and education, and ensure that public services are accessible, transparent, and equitable.

Step 5: Implement Sustainability Features

Design your smart city to be sustainable, incorporating green infrastructure, renewable energy sources, and waste reduction strategies. Use AI to optimize energy consumption, reduce emissions, and promote a circular economy.

Step 6: Present the Prototype

Once the design is complete, present your smart city prototype. Include visual representations, diagrams, and descriptions of the technologies and systems that make up your city. Highlight how these innovations work together to create a more efficient, sustainable, and livable urban environment.

This hands-on project provides an opportunity to apply the concepts and technologies explored in this chapter to create a vision of the future smart city. By integrating emerging technologies like 5G, blockchain, edge computing, and AI, you'll be able to design a city that addresses current challenges while enhancing urban life for residents. Through this project, you gain practical experience in imagining and shaping the cities of tomorrow.

www.ingramcontent.com/pod-product-compliance
Lightning Source LLC
LaVergne TN
LVHW051443050326
832903LV00030BD/3223